ROUTLEDGE LIBRARY EDITIONS:
INDUSTRIAL ECONOMICS

Volume 5

ESTIMATION OF ECONOMIES OF
SCALE IN NINETEENTH CENTURY
UNITED STATES MANUFACTURING

ESTIMATION OF ECONOMIES OF SCALE IN NINETEENTH CENTURY UNITED STATES MANUFACTURING

JEREMY ATACK

LONDON AND NEW YORK

First published in 1985 by Garland Publishing, Inc.

This edition first published in 2018
by Routledge
2 Park Square, Milton Park, Abingdon, Oxon OX14 4RN

and by Routledge
711 Third Avenue, New York, NY 10017

Routledge is an imprint of the Taylor & Francis Group, an informa business

© 1985 Jeremy Atack

All rights reserved. No part of this book may be reprinted or reproduced or utilised in any form or by any electronic, mechanical, or other means, now known or hereafter invented, including photocopying and recording, or in any information storage or retrieval system, without permission in writing from the publishers.

Trademark notice: Product or corporate names may be trademarks or registered trademarks, and are used only for identification and explanation without intent to infringe.

British Library Cataloguing in Publication Data
A catalogue record for this book is available from the British Library

ISBN: 978-1-138-30830-5 (Set)
ISBN: 978-1-351-21102-4 (Set) (ebk)
ISBN: 978-1-138-56712-2 (Volume 5) (hbk)
ISBN: 978-1-315-12409-4 (Volume 5) (ebk)

Publisher's Note
The publisher has gone to great lengths to ensure the quality of this reprint but points out that some imperfections in the original copies may be apparent.

Disclaimer
The publisher has made every effort to trace copyright holders and would welcome correspondence from those they have been unable to trace.

ESTIMATION OF ECONOMIES OF SCALE IN NINETEENTH CENTURY UNITED STATES MANUFACTURING

Jeremy Atack

Garland Publishing, Inc.
New York & London ★ 1985

Copyright © 1985 Jeremy Atack

All rights reserved

Library of Congress Cataloging in Publication Data
Atack, Jeremy.
　Estimation of economies of scale in nineteenth century United States manufacturing.

　(American economic history)
　Revision of the author's thesis (Ph.D.)—Indiana University, 1976.
　Bibliography: p.
　1. United States—Manufactures—History—19th century. 2. Economies of scale—United States—History—19th century. I. Title. II. Series; American economic history (New York, N.Y.)
HD9725.A78　1985　　338.4'767'0973　　84-48303
ISBN 0-8240-6651-0

All volumes in this series are printed on acid-free, 250-year-life paper.

Printed in the United States of America

ESTIMATION OF ECONOMIES OF SCALE IN
NINETEENTH CENTURY UNITED STATES MANUFACTURING

by

Jeremy Atack

CONTENTS

	Page
Table of Contents	iii
List of Tables	v
List of Figures	vii
Preface	viii

1. On the Historical Significance of Economies of Scale 1
   The Role of Constant Returns in Current Historiography .. 1
   Economies of Scale in Current Historiography 3
   The Russel-Linden-Genovese Hypothesis 5

2. On the Estimation of Economies of Scale 12
   Statistical Production Functions 14
     Identification, Bias and Consistency 15
     Estimating Equations 27
   Statistical Cost Functions 35
   The Survivor Techniques 36

3. The Data and Tests of the Samples 40
   The Data 40
   Selection Criteria 48
   Tests of the Samples 48
     Accuracy of the Published Census 49
     One Hundred Percent Samples 49
       California, 1850 50
       Florida, 1850 50
       Oregon, 1850 53
       Oregon, 1860 54
       Texas, 1850 54
     The Samples as a Whole 55
     Representativeness of the Samples 56
     Distribution of Firms by Industry 57
     t-Tests on Firm Statistics 62
   Other Variables 72
     Capital 72
     Labor 76
     Measurement of Output 78

4. The Econometric Interpretation of the Production Function Estimates 82

5. Production Conditions for Intra-Regionally Traded Commodities .. 89
   Flour Milling 92
   Lumber Milling 99

		Page
6.	Production Conditions for Inter-Regionally Traded Commodities .	105
	Boots and Shoes	108
	Clothing	112
	Cotton Textiles	116
7.	The Aggregate Regional Production Function	121
	Census Year 1850	121
	Census Year 1860	123
	Census Year 1870	126
8.	The Sensitivity of Returns to Scale to Units and Methods of Measurement	129
	Sensitivity to the Measurement of Capital	130
	Sensitivity to the Measurement of Labor	133
	Sensitivity to the Measurement of Output	136
9.	Some Evidence on Decreasing Scale Elasticity	140
	Intra-Regionally Traded Commodities	146
	Inter-Regionally Traded Commodities	152
10.	The Survivor Technique and Optimal Plant Size	156
	Application of the Technique to Nineteenth Century Data .	160
	Regional Overview 1850-1870	162
	Optimal Plant Sizes by Industry and Region	167
	Intra-Regionally Traded Commodities	167
	Inter-Regionally Traded Commodities	168
11.	Conclusions	177
	Footnotes to Chapter 1	180
	Footnotes to Chapter 2	183
	Footnotes to Chapter 3	186
	Footnotes to Chapter 4	187
	Footnotes to Chapter 5	188
	Footnotes to chapter 6	189
	Footnotes to Chapter 7	190
	Footnotes to Chapter 8	191
	Footnotes to Chapter 9	192
	Footnotes to Chapter 10	193
	Bibliography	194
	Appendix	210

LIST OF TABLES

		Page
2.1	Bias and Consistency in the Estimation of Returns to Scale	23
2.2	Summary of Estimated Forms of the Production Function	34
3.1	Peculiarities in, and Omissions from, the Sampling Procedure	41
3.2	Sample Sizes and Sampling Proportions: 1850, 1860 and 1870	43
3.3	A Comparison of One Hundred Percent Samples with the Published Census Results	51
3.4	Goodness of Fit and the Industrial Distribution of Firms	58
3.5	Aggregate Mean Values of Sample Statistics, 1850	64
3.6	Aggregate Mean Values of Sample Statistics, 1860	67
3.7	Aggregate Mean Values of Sample Statistics, 1870	70
3.8	Mean Parameters for Twelve Selected Industry Groups from the 1890 Census by Region	74
5.1	The Relative Importance of Local and Regional Manufacturing Industries in the U.S., 1850-1870	90
5.2	Ordinary Least Squares Estimates of the Production Function for Flour Milling, 1850	95
5.3	Ordinary Least Squares Estimates of the Production Function for Flour Milling, 1860	96
5.4	Ordinary Least Squares Estimates of the Production Function for Flour Milling, 1870	97
5.5	Ordinary Least Squares Estimates of the Production Function for Lumber Milling, 1850	101
5.6	Ordinary Least Squares Estimates of the Production Function for Lumber Milling, 1860	102
5.7	Ordinary Least Squares Estimates of the Production Function for Lumber Milling, 1870	103
6.1	Ordinary Least Squares Estimates of the Production Function for Boots and Shoes, 1850	109
6.2	Ordinary Least Squares Estimates of the Production Function for Boots and Shoes, 1860	110
6.3	Ordinary Least Squares Estimates of the Production Function for Boots and Shoes, 1870	111
6.4	Ordinary Least Squares Estimates of the Production Function for Clothing, 1850	113
6.5	Ordinary Least Squares Estimates of the Production Function for Clothing, 1860	114
6.6	Ordinary Least Squares Estimates of the Production Function for Clothing, 1870	115
6.7	Ordinary Least Squares Estimates of the Production Function for Cotton Goods, 1850	117
6.8	Ordinary Least Squares Estimates of the Production Function for Cotton Goods, 1860	118

		Page
6.9	Ordinary Least Squares Estimates of the Production Function for Cotton Goods, 1870	119
7.1	Ordinary Least Squares Estimates of the Aggregate Production Function for Each Region, 1850	122
7.2	Ordinary Least Squares Estimates of the Aggregate Production Function for Each Region, 1860	124
7.3	Ordinary Least Squares Estimates of the Aggregate Production Function for Each Region, 1870	127
8.1	Sensitivity Analysis of Changes in the Measurement of Capital	131
8.2	Sensitivity Analysis of Changes in the Measurement of Labor	134
8.3	Sensitivity of the Returns to Scale Parameter to Changes in the Measurement of Output	137
9.1	Variable Scale Elasticity Production Function Estimates for Intra-Regionally Traded Commodities	147
9.2	The Implied Shape of the Long-Run Average Cost Curve from Variable Scale Elasticity Produciton Function Estimates	149
9.3	Variable Scale Elasticity Production Function Estimates for Inter-Regionally Traded Commodities	153
10.1	Size Categories	161
10.2	Optimal Size Categories of Plant and Minimum Efficient Plant Size by Region	163
10.3	Optimal Size Categories of Plant and Minimum Efficient Plant Size by Region for Flour Milling	169
10.4	Optimal Size Categories of Plant and Minimum Efficient Plant Size by Region for Lumber Milling	170
10.5	Optimal Size Categories of Plant and Minimum Efficient Plant Size by Region for Boots and Shoes	171
10.6	Optimal Size Categories of Plant and Minimum Efficient Plant Size by Region for Clothing	172
10.7	Optimal Size Categories of Plant and Minimum Efficient Plant Size by Region for Cotton Goods	173

LIST OF FIGURES

		Page
1.1	Internal and External Economies of Scale	8
4.1	Monopsony in the Labor Market	86
9.1	Plot of $(\log \hat{\ell} - \log \hat{\ell}_{max})$ for Southern Flour Milling in 1850	145
9.2	Variable Scale Elasticity with Value-Added in Flour Milling in the Southern States in 1850	150
9.3	Variable Scale Elasticity with Value-Added in Flour Milling in the Middle Atlantic States in 1850	151

PREFACE

This work first appeared as my Ph.D. dissertation written at Indiana University in 1975 and 1976 under the title "Estimation and Economies of Scale in Nineteenth Century United States Manufacturing and the Form of the Production Function." Since then it has been substantially revised and abridged as a result of more thought on the subject and with the benefits of hindsight. Changes have been made to reorganize the material from a chronological approach to a topical approach, to delete all discussion of production functions at a more micro-level than a regional four-digit SIC (Standard Industrial Classification) level, and to make the discussion of the historical consistency, significance, and importance of the results explicit rather than implicit. On the other hand, this revision contains little or nothing that is not in the thesis while retaining the results from the thesis and sufficient evidence to support them. The final product is, I hope, a more coherent and engaging piece because it is shorter and less unashamedly quantitative than its precursor.

I would like to thank Stuart Bruchey, editor of this series for soliciting my contribution and for affording me the opportunity to make these revisions.

This work owes much to the members of my thesis committee, Professors Fred Bateman, Clarence Morrison, Gary M. Walton and the late James G. Witte who assisted me by their careful reading and critical comments. Fred Bateman, however, bore the brunt of the work as my thesis chairman. My intellectual development as an economic historian owes a great deal to his inspiration, enthusiasm, guidance and counsel. I owe him a debt that I can never repay.

Fred Bateman also employed me as his research assistant on the National Science Foundation collaborative research project with Professor Thomas Weiss of the University of Kansas into the development of manufacturing industry in mid-nineteenth century America. The pay carried me through the lean years as a graduate student at Indiana University and the experience I gained as their R.A. has proved invaluable. I could not have written my thesis without their help and their selfless interest in my use of the data from the manuscripts of the federal censuses of manufactures for 1850, 1860, and 1870. These data form the backbone of this study.

The computations for this work were for the most part made on the CDC 6600 at the Wrubel Computing Center of Indiana University, though a few of the results are more recent and were made at the University of Illinois Digital Computation Laboratories. I would like to thank both institutions for their generous allocations of computer funds and time. Typing services were provided by the College of Commerce and Business Administration. I thank them for their help.

Jeremy Atack
University of Illinois
March 1984

CHAPTER 1

ON THE HISTORICAL SIGNIFICANCE OF ECONOMIES OF SCALE

On economies of scale during the nineteenth century, much is written and assumed, but little is known. My study seeks to close this gap in our knowledge by providing comprehensive empirical evidence on the status of economies of scale in mid-nineteenth century manufacturing industry. This evidence is in the form of production function estimates made using data from the manuscripts of the federal censuses of manufacturing for 1850, 1860, and 1870. This chapter summarizes the assumptions and evidence on scale economies and addresses some of the specific issues to be resolved with the results presented herein. Chapter 2 outlines the methods of estimation used to derive these. This is followed by a discussion of the data sources and of the problems that are encountered when using census data, especially published census data. The third chapter is therefore likely to be of more general interest. The remainder of the work analyzes and discusses the results.

I. The Role of Constant Returns to Scale in Current Historiography

Probably the most widespread assumption on scale economies in the nineteenth century is of their absence, that is, of the presence of constant returns to scale. No evidence is usually offered in support of this. It is merely asserted that it was so. This assumption is most characteristic of theoretical works where it is a necessary condition for perfect competition or where it is needed for proportionality.

Thus, this assumption plays an essential role in the debate over the effects of abundant land (or of labor scarcity) on American manufacturing and technology.[1] It is the assumption of homogeneity of degree one in the production function[2] that permits Temin to conclude that given the capital-labor ratio, the interest rate is determined and vice versa,[3] but this assumption is essential to all studies of labor (and capital) scarcity.

Constant returns to scale also figure prominently in model building exercises such as that by Williamson.[4] In such models, perfect competition is a necessary condition for resource transfer between sectors and occupations and also to determine factor shares. Indeed, it was to find an empirical basis for income distribution that the Cobb-Douglas production function was first used.[5]

Neither the work on labor scarcity nor that on general equilibrium offers evidence in support of the assumption of constant returns to scale, although, if pressed on the point, the authors would probably cite contemporary evidence on scale economies in the twentieth century. The Walters' survey for example reports the results of fourteen time series which may be "interpreted as confirmation that the aggregate production function has constant returns to scale."[6] Further Walters reports the results of a small number of inter-firm estimates of the production function, concluding that "evidence of constant returns to scale is quite strong."[7]

More recent time series studies notably those by Brown and Popkin[8] and by Bodkin and Klein[9] have shown significant increasing returns to scale. Although Brown and Popkin caution their estimates of economies of scale have an upward bias, their study shows significant increasing returns to scale for the period 1890-1918, constant or marginally decreasing returns in the period 1918-1935, and constant returns to scale for the period 1935-1958.[10] Bodkin and Klein also found evidence of increasing returns to scale for the period 1909-1949.[11]

Since the publication of the Walters' survey the focus of cross-sectional and interindustry studies has shifted and it now concentrates on data from the 1958 Census of Manufactures. However, the results are inconclusive, largely as a result of differing estimation procedures and the measurement of the relevant variables. Both Hildebrand and Liu[12] and Griliches[13] conclude that "there appear to be indications of definite, even if not particularly large, economies of scale in U.S. Manufacturing."[14] On the other hand, Besen,[15] Ferguson[16] and Moroney[17] conclude that "on balance the hypothesis of constant returns to scale cannot be rejected."[18]

II. Economies of Scale in Current Historiography

None of the studies noted above uses data for a period earlier than 1880. Hitherto no study of mid-nineteenth century production functions has been made, despite the "availability" of the relevant micro-economic data in the Censuses of Manufacturing from 1850 onwards.[19]

A number of studies of economies of scale in agriculture have been made. None is satisfactory. Gray[20] and Dickey and Wilson[21] used the survivor technique (the theory of which is described in Chapter 2 below, with results for U.S. manufacturing given in Chapter 10) to identify those size categories of farms that survived market forces and succeeded in increasing their share of value-added or total farm output.[22] Unfortunately, the survivor principle in isolation neither provides a measure of the importance of economies of scale nor even a test for the existence of economies of scale.[23] In particular, we cannot conclude on the basis of Dickey and Wilson's preliminary results that the optimum plantation sizes of at least 24 slaves in the Old South, 49 slaves in the black soil belt counties and 212 slaves in the alluvial counties are determined by production relationships embodied in the returns to scale parameter.

Fogel and Engerman in Time on the Cross[24] demonstrate the existence of modest increasing returns to scale in southern agriculture using the Parker-Gallman sample. Their results suggest that a ten percent increase in all factors of production employed would on average raise output by approximately 10.6 percent.[25] Despite this, however, Fogel and Engerman go on to assume constant returns to scale when they address the issue of the relative efficiency of southern agriculture because constant returns are necessary for the product exhaustion implicit in their approach.[26]

In manufacturing industries, Walsh has laid great stress upon the role played by economies of scale in the development of manufacturing in six Wisconsin counties.[27] Thus, for example, "Racine did not have the necessary local urban market nor the labor threshold to develop economies of scale and high productivity in a variety of industries."[28] While in flour milling "by the late 1850's Racine mills were becoming less able to compete with the economies of scale practiced by their larger Milwaukee counterparts."[29] In Milwaukee "shoe manufacturers were also notable because they were clearly benefiting from economies of scale. In 1860 the three leading firms had a value-added per worker of $932, in contrast to $365 per worker for forty-eight small firms."[30] No empirical basis for these claims is offered.

The work by Paul David on learning by doing in the New England textile mills provides such an empirical basis.[31] Indeed, the precise form of the micro-data used by David is very similar to that used in this study except that David had sufficient observations to run the time series production function estimates, not possible with census data. On the basis of this work, he concluded that "no support for tariff arguments grounded on the existence of significant scale effects can be found...it is seen that the estimated sums of exponents fall in the range between 0.76 and 0.88, well short of the unitary value indicated by the null hypothesis."[32] Despite this result though, David concludes that it is "quite impossible to reject the null hypothesis that there were constant returns to firm scale in this branch of the ante-bellum textile industry."[33]

One of the most fundamental and important statements of scale economies in nineteenth century manufacturing industry, however, concerns the position of southern manufacturing before the Civil War vis à vis industry in the North. I have called this the Russel-Linden-Genovese hypothesis after its most serious proponents and it is this that is to be the central focus of this dissertation.

III. The Russel-Linden-Genovese Hypothesis

Of the many reasons advanced for the relative underdevelopment of southern manufacturing, few have been more pervasive or had a more lasting impact than that first advanced by Robert R. Russel who argued that:

> Population was comparatively sparce in the South,
> distances were great, and means of transportation
> poor. The poorer whites afforded little demand for
> manufactured goods. Neither did the slaves, but
> the masters, who exploited their labor, presumable

compensated for them in this regard. So markets
were too dispersed and inadequate to encourage
large-scale manufacturing.[34]

This same argument was later stressed by Fabian Linden who wrote:

"The scattered unconcentrated quality of Southern
industry handicapped it badly in competition with
the North. To each establishment it meant concrete-
ly a relative increase in the cost of production.
As J. H. Taylor, the treasurer of Graniteville,
pointed out, a superintendent who received a salary
of $12000 to $15000 (sic) a year could manage a
mill of 12000 spindles as efficiently as one of
3000. ...Consequently, New England mills, which
were by 1860 more than twice the size of Southern
factories, could produce cheaply enough to compete
effectively with the cotton states in the home
market."[35] (as published)

However, its most eloquent expression is in the work of Eugene Genovese[36].

In the Genovese hypothesis:

The South was caught in a contradiction similar to
that facing many underdeveloped countries today.
On the one hand, it provided a market for outside
industry. On the other hand, that very market was
too small to sustain industry on a scale large enough
to compete with outsiders who could draw upon wider
markets. ...Plantation slavery then so limited the
purchasing power of the South that it could not sustain much industry. That industry which could be
raised usually lacked a home market of sufficient
scope to permit large-scale operation; the resultant
costs of production were often too high for success
in competition with Northern firms drawing on much
wider markets.[37]

Two non-mutually exclusive economic interpretations of the Russel-Linden-Genovese "Limited-markets" hypothesis can be made.

(1) That the market size for individual firms or products
prevented southern enterprises from producing an output
large enough to reap the benefits of internal economies
of scale, thereby placing them at a price-competitive
disadvantage vis a vis the larger, and hence, lower cost
producers in the North.

(2) That the aggregate market size obstructed the realization of external scale economies by all manufacturing firms in an area, once again resulting in a price-competitive disadvantage.

Southern firms were in general smaller and less numerous than in the developed northern and western states and this differential was increasing between 1850 and 1860. Indeed by 1860 southern cotton mills were less than one-third the size of those in the North and less than half that of cotton mills in the West where cottons were still an "infant" industry.[38] However, this does not constitute prima-facie evidence in favor of either economic interpretation.

Both variants make assumptions regarding the production function and the shape and/or position of the cost curve. Assuming identical technologies throughout the nation, firms in each region would face identical U-shaped long-run average cost curves. In the absence of external economies, all firms would share the same long-run average cost curve, LRAC, but the smaller southern firms would operate at a point such as $\underline{A}$ in Figure 1.1, while the northern firms would be operating at a point such as $\underline{B}$. If there were substantial internal economies of scale, then C_S, the average unit cost of the southern producer, would be significantly greater than C_N, the northern producer's average cost. Pure external economies on the other hand, which are presumably greater in the North than in the South would result in the long-run average cost curve of the northern producer lying everywhere below that of the southern producer at say LRAC'. However, since we know that in general northern firms were larger than their southern counterparts the northern manufacturer would be operating at point $\underline{B}'$ incurring costs of C_N' rather than at $\underline{A}'$. Hence the northern producer could absorb transportation and

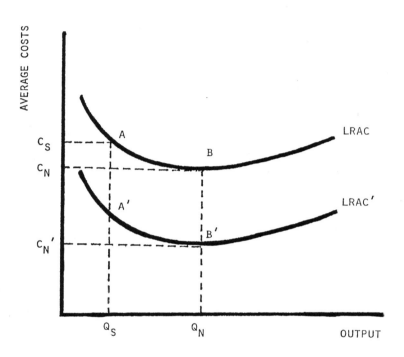

FIGURE 1.1: INTERNAL AND EXTERNAL ECONOMIES OF SCALE

other distribution costs equal up to an amount $C_S - C_N$ or $C_S - C_N'$, depending upon whether there existed only internal economies of scale or whether superimposed over these economies there were additional external economies to be realized, and still deliver the product to a southern market at a price equal to or below that which the southern firm would find profitable in the long run.

Contemporary statements do not universally support the contention of southern inability to be price competitive with northern manufactures either in the South or in other markets. For example, Governor James Hammond,[39] in his probably over-optimistic address to the South Carolina Institute, claimed, "Already the South, through the almost unnoticed enterprise of a few of her citizens more than supplies her own consumption of course (sic) cottons, and ships both yarns and cloths with fair profit to northern markets...we have driven [the northern states] from our markets and have already commenced the contest with them for their own in the only class of goods we have yet attempted."

Notwithstanding the difficulty in interpreting whether Russel, Linden and Genovese perceived economies of scale as internal or external or a combination of the two, there are three fundamental implicit assumptions in their hypothesis:

(1) Given the level of technology, there existed substantial economies of scale in antebellum manufacturing;

(2) Large plant sizes were necessary to realize these scale economies;

(3) Southern firms being smaller, as a consequence operated under increasing returns to scale and decreasing unit cost while northern enterprises produced under conditions of constant returns to scale and constant unit cost, having exploited all potential scale economies.

A slightly weaker version of (3) would assert that while all manufacturing industry had unexploited scale economies, northern firms were able to capture more of their potential than those in the South.

To test the three assumptions implicit in the Russel-Linden-Genovese argument we posit the following three null hypotheses corresponding to these assumptions:

(a) Over some range of outputs, there existed returns to scale that were significantly greater than unity;

(b) Only large firms produced under conditions where the returns to scale were not significantly different from unity;

(c) Firms in the South produced where returns to scale were significantly greater than unity, while Northern firms produced where returns to scale were not significantly different from unity.

Nonrejection of any of these null hypotheses implies nonrejection of that particular assumption in the Russel-Linden-Genovese hypothesis. These tests require estimates of the economies of scale for the "typical" antebellum manufacturing establishment in a particular region or industry, together with estimates of how these economies of scale varied with the size of the establishment.

I will examine the quantitative evidence on the existence or nonexistence of unexploited scale economies in antebellum manufacturing and the support for the three underlying assumptions in the Russel-Linden-Genovese thesis. Attention is not confined to a North-South comparison, although this has been the thrust of those who would emphasize southern backwardness, for as Fogel and Engerman[40] point out the question is, "if the South was a poverty-ridden 'colonial dependency', how are we to characterize the states that occupy the territory running from the western border of Pennsylvania to the western border of Nebraska--states usually thought of as examples of high prosperity and rapid growth during the antebellum era?"

While the results for 1870 do not fit into this scheme, they are included because they represent important evidence on production relationships on the eve of the emergence of big business. They can thus be used to judge whether the incipient merger movement and growth of bigness had its roots in unrealized scale economies.

CHAPTER 2

ON THE ESTIMATION OF ECONOMIES OF SCALE

Let us assume that for any particular industry there exists some well defined relationship between output, Q and inputs, X: Q=f(X). This relationship is known as the production function and characterizes the efficient production set by specifying the maximum attainable output given any inputs. Ex ante selection of a production function is determined by the available technology, the set of market prices facing the firm and entrepreneurial expectations of the potential demand.[1] Ex post under conditions of imperfect foresight and adaptability, the attainment of that output level specified by the ex ante production function is an unlikely event. This distinction between the ex ante production function and the ex post production relationship is crucial and provides a rationale for the statistical estimation of the production function.

Generally speaking, the production function has three parameters of interest:

(1) the elasticity of output with respect to particular inputs, $\alpha_i = (\partial Q/\partial X_i) \cdot (X_i/Q)$,

(2) the degree of homogeneity of the production function, or the elasticity of scale, $\varepsilon = \Sigma \alpha_i$, that is the elasticity of output with respect to a proportional change in all inputs, and

(3) the elasticity of substitution, σ, between inputs.

The elasticity of substitution measures the curvature of the isoquants for a particular input combination and hence the rate at which they can be substituted for one another. For two input factors, X_1 and X_2, the elasticity of substitution is defined as:

$$\sigma(X_1, X_2) = \left. \frac{\frac{X_2}{X_1} \cdot d\left(\frac{X_1}{X_2}\right)}{\frac{f_1}{f_2} \cdot d\left(\frac{f_2}{f_1}\right)} \right|_{\text{Output} = \text{Constant}}$$

where $f_i = \partial F/\partial X_i$ is the marginal productivity of the i-the factor. Unfortunately it is difficult to generalize the elasticity of the substitution to more than two input factors without imposing additional constraints on the remaining variables in addition to the constraint on output. The elasticity of substitution between any two input factors will vary depending on the constraints imposed upon the remaining (n-2) factors.[2] This clearly limits the usefulness of the elasticity of substitution. Fortunately, the elasticity of substitution is not vital in this study and is only of peripheral importance.

In contrast, the output elasticities and the elasticity of scale are readily generalized to any number of factors of production and are central to this study. The output elasticities provide us with a normalized (independent of the units of measurement) measure of the importance of any particular factor in the production process. Furthermore, under conditions of perfect competition and constant returns to scale, the output elasticities correspond to the factor shares of total output and measure the marginal productivities of those factors of production.

The scale elasticity, given by the sum of the output elasticities, measures the relative increase in output for a given proportional change in all inputs and at any point they are said to be decreasing, constant or increasing returns to scale according to whether the elasticity of scale is less than, equal to, or greater than unity.

If one had prior information about the relationship between these three elasticities and inputs then a production function incorporating these properties could be devised. For example, Kmenta and Joseph using Monte Carlo techniques concluded that the "choice of an estimation method has to depend on the specific field of application and on the knowledge of the technical and economic characteristics of the industry."[3] If such knowledge were available, then the only matter of interest would be to explain the deviations of the observed outputs from those predicted. Unfortunately, "significant knowledge of the relevant technical and economic characteristics of an industry will come after, and not before, statistical estimation."[4] The task therefore becomes one of both estimating the parameters of the production function and rationalizing the "errors" in the predictions.

I. Statistical Production Functions

Of the many techniques that have been used to estimate the relevant parameters of the production function, none has been used more extensively nor aroused more criticism than the statistical estimation of the production function using regression analysis. Critics have concentrated their attack on three critical issues: identification, bias and consistency.

A. Identification, Bias and Consistency

Following Marschak and Andrews[5] and assuming for simplicity a Cobb-Douglas production function, the neoclassical theory of the firm assumes that firms maximize profits subject to their production function constraint:

maximize: $\pi = p \cdot Q - r \cdot K - w \cdot L$ [2.1] Profit Definition

subject to: $Q = A \cdot L^\alpha \cdot K^\beta$ [2.2] Production Function

where K and L represent the inputs of capital and labor, r and w are their respective market prices, Q is output and is sold for price, p and π is profit defined as the difference between total revenues and total costs. Forming the Lagrange multiplier:

maximize $(\pi) = p \cdot Q - r \cdot K - w \cdot L - \lambda(Q-f)$ [2.3]

where $f = A \cdot L^\alpha \cdot K^\beta$, then first order conditions for a maximum require that:

$$\frac{\partial \pi}{\partial Q} = p - \lambda = 0 \quad [2.4]$$

$$\frac{\partial \pi}{\partial L} = \lambda f_L - w = 0 \quad [2.5]$$

$$\frac{\partial \pi}{\partial K} = \lambda f_K - r = 0 \quad [2.6]$$

$$\frac{\partial \pi}{\partial \lambda} = Q - f = 0 \quad [2.7]$$

which imply that:

$$p = \lambda \qquad [2.8]$$

$$w = \lambda f_L \qquad [2.9]$$

$$r = \lambda f_K \qquad [2.10]$$

$$Q = f \qquad [2.11]$$

The marginal productivities of labor and capital are f_L and f_K respectively:

$$f_L = \frac{\partial Q}{\partial L} = \alpha \cdot \frac{Q}{L} \qquad [2.12] \text{ from } [2.2]$$

$$f_K = \frac{\partial Q}{\partial K} = \beta \cdot \frac{Q}{K} \qquad [2.13] \text{ from } [2.3]$$

But:

$$f_L = \frac{w}{p} \qquad [2.9']$$

and $$f_K = \frac{r}{p} \qquad [2.10']$$

Therefore, the full production model may be written as:

$$Q = A \cdot L^\alpha \cdot K^\beta \qquad [2.2]: \text{ Supply of output}$$

$$\frac{w}{p} = \alpha \cdot \frac{Q}{L} \qquad [2.14]: \text{ Demand for labor, from } [2.9']$$
$$\text{and } [2.12]$$

$$\frac{r}{p} = \beta \cdot \frac{Q}{K} \qquad [2.15]: \text{ Demand for capital, from}$$
$$[2.10'] \text{ and } [2.13]$$

Performing a logarithmic transformation this system of simultaneous equations yields:

$$\begin{rcases} X_0 - \alpha X_1 - X\beta_2 = \lambda_0 \\ X_0 - X_1 = \lambda_0 \\ X_0 - X_2 = \lambda_3 \end{rcases} \quad [2.16]$$

where:

$$X_0 = \log Q;$$
$$X_1 = \log L;$$
$$X_2 = \log K;$$
$$\lambda_0 = \log A;$$
$$\lambda_1 = \log \frac{w}{\alpha \cdot p};$$
$$\lambda_2 = \log \frac{r}{\beta \cdot p};$$

or more compactly in matrix form:

$$\begin{bmatrix} X_0 \\ X_1 \\ X_2 \end{bmatrix} = \begin{bmatrix} 1 & -\alpha & -\beta \\ 1 & -1 & 0 \\ 1 & 0 & -1 \end{bmatrix}^{-1} \begin{bmatrix} \lambda_0 \\ \lambda_1 \\ \lambda_2 \end{bmatrix} \quad [2.17]$$

For a given set of prices, p, r and w, this system of simultaneous equations [2.17] will generate a single point on the firm's production function. Obviously, the production function would not be identified. If, however, prices vary over time, then the production function for the firm will be identified. Alternatively, under the assumptions of perfect competition and knowledge, the vector of prices facing each firm is fixed. Therefore, if each firm was subject to the same production function, each would produce exactly the same quantity of output and once again the production function would not be identified.

Suppose, however, that entrepreneurial talent was distributed randomly throughout the population of firms. Then, while still maintaining the assumption of perfect competition, the production function for the i-th firm could be written as:

$$Q_i = A_i \cdot L_i^\alpha \cdot K_i^\beta \qquad [2.18]$$

where

$$A_i = Ae^{u_{0i}} \qquad [2.19]$$

and u_i is a random variable, that is, firms differ from one another with respect to the technical ability of their entrepreneur. Hence each firm will have a different coefficient of technical efficiency, A_i. Similarly, differences in the technological embodiment of the inherited capital would manifest themselves as changes in A_i. However, technological embodiment is assumed constant over time. Because of these differences it is also reasonable to assume that individual entrepreneurial reactions to the given market set of prices will vary.

Therefore, for the i-th firm, [2.17] may be written as:

$$\begin{bmatrix} X_{0i} \\ X_{1i} \\ X_{2i} \end{bmatrix} = \begin{bmatrix} 1 & -\alpha & -\beta \\ 1 & -1 & 0 \\ 1 & 0 & -1 \end{bmatrix}^{-1} \begin{bmatrix} \lambda_0 & u_{0i} \\ \lambda_1 & u_{1i} \\ \lambda_2 & u_{2i} \end{bmatrix} \qquad [2.20]$$

where u_{1i} and u_{2i} are stochastic variables representing the differing economic abilities of the entrepreneurs.

Suppose further that firms are unable to satisfy their marginal productivity constraints exactly due to market imperfections or the inability of the firm to adapt instantaneously to a new vector of prices because of the inherited stock of labor and/or capital. Equations [2.9] and [2.10] may therefore be written as:

$$R_1 w = \lambda f_L \qquad [2.21]$$

$$R_2 r = \lambda f_K \qquad [2.22]$$

Substituting [2.21] and [2.22] into [2.12] and [2.13] yields the following set of simultaneous equations:

$$\begin{bmatrix} X_{0i} \\ X_{1i} \\ X_{2i} \end{bmatrix} = \begin{bmatrix} 1 & -\alpha & -\beta \\ 1 & -1 & 0 \\ 1 & 0 & -1 \end{bmatrix}^{-1} \begin{bmatrix} \lambda_0 & u_{0i} \\ \lambda_1 & u_{1i} \\ \lambda_2 & u_{2i} \end{bmatrix} \qquad [2.23]$$

where $\lambda_1 = \ln \dfrac{R_1 w}{\alpha \cdot p}$ and $\lambda = \ln \dfrac{R_2 r}{\beta \cdot p}$.

For cross-sectional data, under the assumption of a fixed vector prices, λ_0, λ_1 and λ_2 will be constants and once again the production function will not be identified since the system has no exogenous variables. Furthermore, it is highly probable that variations in entrepreneurial technical expertise (u_0), will be positively correlated with variations in entrepreneurial economic expertise (u_1 and u_2). Consequently the equations of [2.23] will not be independent and the regression estimates will be biased and inconsistent.

Fortunately, Zellner, Kmenta and Dreze[6] have developed an alternative specification of the model which circumvents these problems. The principal distinction between the Zellner et al. model and that developed by Marschak and Andrews is that Zellner et al. recognize that the production process is not instantaneous and that entrepreneurs as a consequence operate under conditions of uncertainty. Firms therefore attempt to maximize expected profit and the production function is disturbed by factors beyond the control of the entrepreneur, such as weather or unpredictable variations in machine or labor performance, which are not known with certainty until after the production process is completed. Furthermore, Zellner et al. assume that prices are either known with certainty or that they are statistically independent of the production function with expectations p*, r* and w* for the i-th firm. It should be noted that, under conditions of imperfect competition, prices are a function of the quantity sold or purchased so that $E(p \cdot Q) \neq p^* \cdot E(Q)$[7] where p is the price of output (resource), p* is the expected price, and Q is the quantity sold (purchased). However, neglecting this distinction, the model [2.1] and [2.2] may be rewritten as:

$$\text{max:} \quad E(\pi) = p^* \cdot E(Q) - w^* \cdot L - r^* \cdot K \quad [2.24]$$

$$\text{subject to:} \quad E(Q) = A \cdot L^\alpha \cdot K^\beta e^{1/2(\sigma_{00}^2)} \quad [2.25]$$

where σ_{00}^2 is the variance of the normally distributed production function disturbance, u_0. Disturbances of the production function in this model clearly affect the ability of the firm to meet its marginal productivity constraints. However, it is also probable that the marginal productivity constraints will be disturbed by the ex post differences between expected and realized prices. Therefore, in matrix form after logarithmic transformations, the Zellner et al. model may be written as:

$$\begin{bmatrix} X_0 \\ X_1 \\ X_2 \end{bmatrix} = \begin{bmatrix} 1 & -\alpha & -\beta \\ 1 & -1 & 0 \\ 1 & 0 & -1 \end{bmatrix}^{-1} \begin{bmatrix} \lambda_0 & u_0 & 0 \\ \lambda_1 & u_0 & u_1 \\ \lambda_2 & u_0 & u_2 \end{bmatrix} \quad [2.26]$$

where u_1 and u_2 disappear if prices are known with certainty and

$$\lambda_1 = \{\log \frac{wR_1}{\alpha \cdot p}\}^{-1/2\sigma_{00}}$$

and $\quad \lambda_2 = \{\log \frac{rR_2}{\beta \cdot p}\}^{-1/2\sigma_{00}}$.

All other symbols have the same meaning as in (2.A.16). The production function is identified.

Given the interpretation accorded the disturbance terms, u_0, ('acts of God') and u_1 and u_2 ('human error') in this model, it is reasonable to assume that the correlation between u_o and u_1 and between u_0 and u_2 is zero. Consequently not only is the system of simultaneous equations [2.26] consistent, but also simple least squares estimation of:

$$X_0 = \lambda_0 + \alpha X_1 + \beta X_2 + u_0 \quad [2.27]$$

the log transformation of the Cobb-Douglas production function (the first equation of [2.26], will also be consistent. Furthermore, if it is assumed that u_1 and u_2 are normally distributed, or that u_1 and u_2 are statistically independent of u_0, then ordinary least squares estimates (OLS) of [2.27] will be unbiased.[8]

There have been a number of empirical studies on the bias and consistency of alternative specifications of the production function and their principal results are summarized in Table 2.1. Maddala and Kadane[9] investigated the bias and consistency in the estimation of scale elasticity with respect to variations in the elasticity of substitution. Using Monte Carlo methods, they fitted an unconstrained Cobb-Douglas production function, for which, by definition the elasticity of substitution is equal to unity, while supposing that the 'true' underlying production function was a CES function with constant returns to scale. They concluded that if capital and labor were independent log-normal, then there was no appreciable bias in the estimate of the returns to scale parameter for wide variations in the elasticity of substitution. Bodkin and Klein[10] have reported estimates of the scale elasticity for the period 1909-1949. Their estimates using simple regression and simultaneous equation estimation of Cobb-Douglas and CES production functions with both additive and multiplicative error specifications are also remarkably consistent. Finally, Kmenta and Joseph,[11] using Monte Carlo techniques tested the bias of five estimation techniques in nine separate models for two sample sizes. The results and their implications for empirical research are discouraging. They conclude that:

> No single estimation procedure is satisfactory in all circumstances. Ordinary least squares estimates tend to have an upward bias; Klein's estimates, though highly efficient, are biased in the absence of effective profit maximization; and Hoch's, and to some extent indirect least squares estimates, can be highly unstable in small samples.[12]

Table 2.1

Bias and Consistency in the Estimation of Returns to

Scale from Statistical Production Functions

Study/Assumptions	Returns to Scale Actual	Estimated	Bias
I. Maddala and Kadane:			
K and L Uniform Distribution			
$\sigma = 0.3$	1.00	1.40*	.40
$\sigma = 0.7$	1.00	1.17*	.17
$\sigma = 1.6$	1.00	0.82**	-.18
$\sigma = 2.5$	1.00	0.75**	-.25
K and L Lognormal			
$\sigma = 0.3$	1.00	1.05	.05
$\sigma = 0.7$	1.00	1.06	.06
$\sigma = 1.6$	1.00	1.01	.01
$\sigma = 2.5$	1.00	1.02	.02
Kmenta's Approximation, K and L Lognormal[1]			
$\sigma = 0.4$	0.40	0.38	-.02
	0.90	0.92	.02
	1.60	1.63	.03
	2.50	2.50	.00
$\sigma = 0.9$	0.40	0.42	.02
	0.90	0.91	.01
	1.60	1.60	.00
	2.50	2.46	-.04
$\sigma = 1.6$	0.40	0.39	-.01
	0.90	0.92	.02
	1.60	1.54	-.06
	2.50	2.46	-.04
$\sigma = 2.5$	0.40	0.38	-.02
	0.90	0.92	.02
	1.60	1.59	-.01
	2.50	2.50	.00

Table 2.1 continued

Model/Assumptions	Sample Size	Returns to Scale Actual	Estimated	Bias
II. Kmenta and Joseph Model D[2]				
Ordinary Least Squares	20	0.9	0.95	.05
	100	0.9	0.95	.05
Hoch's Estimate for Uncorrelated Errors[3]	20	0.9	0.95	.05
	100	0.9	0.95	.05
Hoch's Estimate for Partly Correlated Errors[3]	20	0.9	0.95	.05
	100	0.9	0.96	.06
Klein[4]	20	0.9	0.90	.00
	100	0.9	0.90	.00
Indirect Least Squares[5]	20	0.9	0.95	.05
	100	0.9	0.95	.05

	Estimating Equation	Returns to Scale
III. Bodkin and Klein		
Straight Regression Multiplicative Errors	CD function	1.20
	CES function	1.21
Straight Regression Additive Errors	CD function	1.21
	CES function	1.22
Simultaneous Equations Multiplicative Errors	CD function[6]	1.46
	CES function[7]	1.24
Simultaneous Equations Additive Errors	CD function[8]	1.47
	CES function[9]	1.36

Notes:

*Estimated coefficient is significantly greater than the actual.

**Estimated coefficient is significantly smaller than the actual.

[1] Variance of the disturbance = 0.1. Maddala and Kadane also report that increasing the variance of the disturbance to 0.4 does not appreciably alter the estimate of the returns to scale parameter.

Footnotes to Table 2.1 continued

[2]The disturbance for Model D are as follows:

$$E(u_2) = .0004$$
$$E(v_1^2) = .0004$$
$$E(v_2^2) = .0004$$
$$E(uv_1) = .0004(\sqrt{.8})$$
$$E(uv_2) = .0004(\sqrt{.8})$$
$$E(v_1 v_2) = .00032$$
$$\rho_{uv_1} = .8$$
$$\rho_{uv_2} = \sqrt{.8}$$
$$\rho_{v_1 v_2} = \sqrt{.8}$$

Where u = technical disturbances (equivalent to u_0 above) and v_1 and u_2 are economic disturbances (equivalent to u_1 and u_2).

[3]See J. Kmenta and M. G. Joseph, (1963), pp. 366-368 for a complete specification of the Hoch Model.

[4]Klein's estimates are based on the assumption that the average firm is optimal (as in Model D). When the average firm is not optimal or if one input is predetermined, Klein's estimates are biased an inconsistent. See Kmenta and Joseph, (1963), p. 369 for a complete specification of the Klein model.

[5]Estimated using indirect least squares on the transformed Cobb-Douglas production function:

$$x_0 = b_0 + b_1 Z_1 + b_2 Z_2 + e$$

where
$$z_r = x_r - x_0$$
$$b_r = a_r/(1 - a_1 - a_2) \quad (r = 1, 2)$$

where economies of scale = $a_1 + a_2$.

[6]Estimated correlation between production function residuals and marginal productivity residuals, $\rho_{uv} = -.0101$.

[7]$\rho_{uv} = -.7524$

Footnotes to Table 2.1 continued

[8] $\rho_{uv} = -.0063$

[9] $\rho_{uv} = -.3575$

<u>Sources</u>: G. S. Maddala and J. B. Kadane (1967).

J. Kmenta and M. G. Joseph, (1963).

R. G. Bodkin and L. R. Klein, (1967).

B. Estimating Equations

Following the Zellner, Kmenta and Dreze model, the principal estimation technique will be simple OLS estimation of an unconstrained Cobb-Douglas production function of the form:

$$\log Q_{ijk} = \log A + \alpha \cdot \log L_{ijk} + \beta \cdot \log K_{ijk} + u_{ijk} \qquad [2.28]$$

where i varies over the firms in an industry, j varies over the industries and k varies over the individual states from which the samples were drawn. It is assumed that the entrepreneurs, recognizing the existence of uncertainty in a non-instantaneous production world, seek to maximize their expected profits, but that the production function is disturbed by random "Acts of God," u_{ijk}. The problems posed by imperfect competition and hence the existence of a transmission mechanism whereby disturbance terms are transmitted from the production function to the marginal productivity constraints as in [2.26] are ignored.

Equation [2.28] provides direct estimates of the output elasticities, α and β, together with tests of their significance. Although this functional form also provides an estimate of the scale elasticity, $\varepsilon = \alpha + \beta$, testing the significance of the scale elasticity is inconvenient due to the non-zero covariance in the ex post production function model. The sample variance of the scale elasticity is:

$$s_\varepsilon^2 = s_\alpha^2 + s_\beta^2 + 2s_{\alpha\beta}$$

For convenience, therefore, a variation on equation [2.28] is also estimated. Given a Cobb-Douglas production function homogeneous of degree $(\alpha+\beta)$:

$$Q = A \cdot L^{\alpha} \cdot K^{\beta}$$

this may be rewritten as:

$$Q/L = A \cdot (K/L)^{\beta} \cdot L^{\xi} \qquad [2.29]$$

where $\xi = \alpha + \beta - 1 = \varepsilon - 1$.[13] Performing a logarithmic transformation on [2.29] yields:

$$\log (Q/L)_{ijk} = \log A + \alpha \cdot \log (K/L)_{ijk} + \xi \cdot \log L_{ijk} + u_{ijk} \qquad [2.30]$$

for the individual firm, where ξ in [2.30] is a direct estimate of the difference of the economies of scale parameter from unity and hence provides a convenient, direct test of the significance of economies of scale for the estimate.

Although the elasticity of substitution is not an issue in this study, the Maddala and Kadane results[14] suggest the wisdom of verifying that variations in the elasticity of substitution from unity will not appreciably bias the returns to scale parameter. Given a CES production function, homogeneous of degree μ,

$$Q = A[\delta K^{-\rho} + (1-\delta) L^{-\rho}]^{-\mu/\rho} \qquad [2.31]$$

this may be rewritten as:

$$Q/L = A \cdot L^{\xi} [\delta (K/L)^{-\rho} + (1-\delta)]^{-\mu/\rho} \qquad [2.32]$$

where $\xi = \mu - 1 = \varepsilon - 1$. Unfortunately the CES production function is not linear in logarithms and hence estimation is both inconvenient and difficult. However, Kmenta[15] has developed an approximation using

Taylor's series expansion of the logarithmic transformation of the function about $\rho = 0$. Performing the transformation on [2.32] yields:

$$\log (Q/L) = \log A + \xi \log L - (\mu/\rho)f(\rho) \qquad [2.33]$$

where $f(\rho) = \log[\delta(K/L)^{-\rho} + (1-\delta)]$.

Expanding $f(\rho)$ around $\rho = 0$:

$$f(\rho) \approx f(0) + f'(0)\rho + \frac{\rho^2}{2} f''(0) + o(\rho)$$

where $f(0) = 0$

$f'(0) = -\delta \log (K/L)$

$f''(0) = \delta(1-\delta)[\log (K/L)]^2$

and $o(\rho) = 0$, that is, third and higher orders are assumed to be zero unless the capital-labor ratio and the elasticity of substitution are either very large or very small.

Thus equation [2.33] becomes:

$$\log (Q/L) \approx \log A + \xi \log L + (\mu/\rho)\rho\delta[\log (K/L)] -$$

$$\frac{(\mu/\rho)\rho^2 \delta(1-\delta)}{2} [\log (K/L)]^2$$

$$\approx \log A + \xi \log L + \mu\delta\log (K/L) - \frac{\mu\rho\delta(1-\delta)}{2} [\log (K/L)]^2$$
$$[2.34]$$

which may be generalized for the i-th firm in the j-th industry located in the k-th state by adding appropriate subscripts and the production function disturbance term, u_{ijk}.

Since the elasticity of substitution, $\sigma = \frac{1}{(1+\rho)}$, if $\rho = 0$, then $\sigma = 1$ and [2.34] reduces to the Cobb-Douglas production function [2.2] since the coefficient of the square of the log [capital-labor] ratio vanishes. *Ceteris paribus*, a significant coefficient of the squared log of the capital-labor ratio indicates a value of ρ significantly different from zero and hence an elasticity of substitution different from unity. If capital and labor follow some distribution other than log-normal, then the returns to scale parameter will be overestimated if ρ is positive and underestimated if ρ is negative. Furthermore this bias may be made arbitrarily large.[16]

However, rejection of the Cobb-Douglas production function if the elasticity of substitution is significantly different from unity does not imply acceptance of the CES form, since an elasticity of substitution different from unity is compatible with many alternative formulations of the production function.[17]

The test, however, is unsatisfactory in many respects. The further away the underlying production function is from the Cobb-Douglas form, the more important the third and higher order terms which are ignored in the Kmenta approximation become. Moreover, the effect of these ignored terms on the coefficient of the squared capital-labor ratio is unpredictable. Additionally, since this coefficient is one half of the product of μ, ρ, δ and $(1-\delta)$, where δ and $(1-\delta)$ are both less than unity, the absolute value of the coefficient will tend to be small.[18] Consequently, in order to obtain reliable tests of the sign and magnitude of the coefficient significant dispersion in the K/L ratio and large samples are necessary. Furthermore, the Kmenta approximation is not in a constant elasticity form and therefore the estimates, ξ, μ, ρ and δ are not independent of the units of measurement. Hence, the elasticity of substitution will not be independent of those units of measurement.[19]

The forms of the production function discussed above belong to a special class of homogeneous and homothetic production functions[20] which is a sub-set of the more general production function model. In particular, the production function model underlying the theory of costs is non-homogeneous. At low levels of output, the firm is generally considered to be operating in the range of increasing returns to scale, while at high levels of output, the theory of cost frequently presumes the existence of decreasing returns to scale. At intermediate levels of output, on the other hand, the firm is generally thought to be operating under constant returns to scale. The estimation of a homogeneous production function unfortunately does not permit such generalization, unless a series of homogeneous production functions are estimated for sub-sets of the data. However, the estimatation of a series of homogeneous production functions for sub-sets of the data is likely to lead to small sample estimation problems. Therefore it is generally preferable to estimate a non-homogeneous production function. A number of alternative formulations of inhomogeneous production functions have been developed.[21]

Non-homogeneity may be expected to manifest itself in second or higher order terms. Therefore, adding second order terms to the Cobb-Douglas production function [2.28] yields:

$$\log Q = \log A + \alpha \log L + \beta \log K + \gamma_{11}(\log L)^2 + \gamma_{12}(\log L \cdot \log K) + \gamma_{22}(\log K)^2 \qquad [2.35]$$

where $\varepsilon = \alpha + \beta + (2\gamma_{11} + \gamma_{12}) \cdot \log L + (2\gamma_{22} + \gamma_{12}) \cdot \log K$

If

$$\gamma_{12} = -2\gamma_{11} = -2\gamma_{22}$$

then equation [2.35] is homogeneous and consequently the elasticity of scale is constant. Furthermore, if $\gamma_{12} = 0$, then [2.35] reduces to [2.28].[22] It should also be noted that [2.35] is a more general formulation of the Kmenta approximation [2.34] and that [2.35] is non-homothetic. Consequently, equation [2.35] may also be used to test the homotheticity of the production function.[23] The production function is homothetic if

$$\gamma_{12} = -2\gamma_{11} = -2\gamma_{22} = 0$$

But, as already pointed out, the elasticity of substitution and hence by implication homotheticity is not an issue in this study. However, nothing is known about the potential bias in the elasticity of scale parameter estimates from a homothetic production function, if the underlying production function is non-homothetic.

The form of the production function underlying Nerlove's study of the electricity generating industry is:[24]

$$\log Q + \phi(\log Q)^2 = \tau \log L + \Omega \log (K/L) \qquad [2.36]$$

which has scale elasticity

$$\varepsilon(Q) = \tau/(1+2\phi \log Q)$$

The production function estimated by Zellner and Revankar[25] is essentially similar:

$$\log Q + \Theta Q = \tau \log L + \Omega \log (K/L) \qquad [2.37]$$

where the elasticity of scale is

$$\varepsilon(Q) = \tau/(1 + \Theta Q).$$

Ringstad has suggested an alternative non-homogeneous production function which is a combination of the Nerlove and Zellner and Revankar production function:[26]

$$\log Q + \phi(\log Q)^2 + \Theta Q = \tau \log L + \Omega \log (K/L) \qquad [2.38]$$

where scale elasticity is

$$\varepsilon(Q) = \tau/(1 + 2\phi \log Q + \Theta Q)$$

Each of these production function forms is homothetic and will exhibit decreasing elasticity of scale provided that $\tau>0$, $\phi>0$ and $\Theta>0$.

The forms of the production function to be estimated are summarized in Table 2.2 Equations [I] - [III] are homogeneous production functions, while equations [IV] - [VII] are non-homogeneous production functions which exhibit decreasing scale elasticity with increasing scale of the enterprise. All estimated production functions with the exception of equation [IV] are also homothetic.

Table 2.2

Summary of Estimated Forms of the Production Function

Equation	Number	Equation Form	Scale Elasticity
[I]	[2.28]	$\log Q = \log A + \alpha \log L + \beta \log K$	$\alpha + \beta$
[II]	[2.30]	$\log(Q/L) = \log A + \xi \log L + \beta \log(K/L)$	$\xi + 1$
[III]	[2.34]	$\log(Q/L) = \log A + \xi \log L + \mu \delta \log(K/L) - 1/2[\mu \rho \delta (1-\delta)(\log(K/L))^2]$	$\xi + 1$
[IV]	[2.35]	$\log Q = \log A + \alpha \log L + \beta \log K + \gamma_{11}(\log L)^2 + \gamma_{12} \log L \cdot \log K + \gamma_{22}(\log K)^2$	$\alpha + \beta + (2\gamma_{11} + \gamma_{12})\log L$ $+ (2\gamma_{22} + \gamma_{12})\log K$
[V]	[2.36]	$\log Q + \phi (\log Q)^2 = \tau \log L + \Omega \log(K/L)$	$\tau/(1 + 2\phi \log Q)$
[VI]	[2.37]	$\log Q + \theta Q = \tau \log L + \Omega \log(K/L)$	$\tau/(1 + \theta Q)$
[VII]	[2.38]	$\log Q + \phi (\log Q)^2 + \theta Q = \tau \log L + \Omega \log(K/L)$	$\tau/(1 + 2\phi \log Q + \theta Q)$

Sources: See Text.

II. Statistical Cost Functions

The discussion in Chapter 1 of the historical importance and significance of economies of scale relied heavily upon references to cost curves. However, cost function estimates will not be made even though they can be derived from the reduced forms of the marginal productivity and production relationships given above in equation [2.17]. This decision not to explicitly estimate cost functions reflects the damaging criticisms made of this method, sketched briefly below, and inadequacies with the data, discussed in Chapter 3.

Under conditions of perfect competition (as defined by economic theory) total revenues are equal to total costs and hence cross-sectional data will tend to give rise to apparently constant average costs. Cross-section data generally lack the needed exogeneous variables such as demand shifts to aid identification. Therefore, in a perfectly competitive industry, variations in output from firm to firm must result from either continuous long-run mistakes or from the control of some specialized resource. Redefining costs to exclude rents to these specialized factors internal to the firm (e.g., extraordinary managerial expertise) merely leads to a regression "explaining" how managerial ability varied with output.[27]

These criticisms, however, do not apply either to time series data, where there is greater justification for the supposition of exogeneous variation to aid identification, or to cross-section data under monopolistic conditions. However, monopolistic elements present their own problems. Product differentiation and varying degree of monopsony in local markets cloud the concept of a cross-sectional cost function for the industry under such conditions.

Interestingly, the principal findings of cost function studies, unlike those of production functions, are not in complete agreement with economic theory. The long-run average cost curve appears to be L-shaped rather than the more commonly assumed U-shape and hence marginal costs have been found to be constant over wide ranges of output. Optimum plant size would therefore appear to be indeterminate.[28] Attempts to rationalize these findings have emphasized three potential sources of bias.[29] First, the use of accounting data, particularly the accounting treatment of depreciation and asset valuation and the non-coincidence of accounting and economic time periods, may introduce spurious linearities. Second, the statistical treatment and processing of time series data using price indices may introduce either linear or curvilinear bias to the results. Third, cross-sectional studies which have no variable cost data may be subject to the regression fallacy. Firms with the largest potential output are unlikely to be producing at low levels, rather they will tend to be producing at unusually high levels and conversely for those firms with the lowest output.[30]

Because of these problems, the cost function approach is not used but interpretation of the production function results will frequently be made in terms of cost curves.

III. The Survivor Technique

George Stigler has suggested an alternative method to the statistical estimation of production or cost functions to identify economies of scale.[31] Publication of his 1958 article "The Economies of Scale" engendered subsequent application of this technique to a wide range of twentieth century industries principally in connection with anti-trust issues.[32] The concept is not new. It can be traced back to John Stuart Mill and to Willard Thorp.

The survivor technique seeks to identify that size of plant or those sizes of plants that, over time, increased their relative contribution to total value-added. Assuming well functioning market mechanisms, economic theory predicts that in the long run, firms will construct optimally sized plants with respect to prevailing cost and demand conditions in order to maximize long-run profits. These optimally sized plants may be all of approximately the same size, or may cover a fairly wide range of plant sizes.

Data inadequacies due to the disclosure laws have generally confounded application of this technique to the twentieth century. In particular, the measurement of plant size by output or value-added is impossible and consequently employment has been used instead as a proxy for size. Only in the absence of innovation or in the present of constant output-labor ratios over time and across plant sizes will estimates of size based upon employment be unbiased. The nineteenth century manuscript data present no such problems, since plant size can be measured by output, value-added, employment or invested capital.

The theory developed by Stigler implicitly assumes perfect competition so that the long-run equilibrium conditions for the firm and industry are satisfied when all plants are of a size consistent with minimum long-run average total cost and all firms are earning only normal profits.

In this particular instance, provided plant size is measured by output or value-added, it is possible to translate the range of optimal plant sizes into a range of constant average costs. Such plants are then optimal not only from the point of view of the firm, since they represent the least cost method of producing a given level of output, but also from the point of view of society.

The article by William Shepherd, "What does the Survivor Technique show about Economics of Scale"[33] identifies three principal advantages of the method. First, "it finesses the problem of the capitalization of rents into costs a process that drives disparate measured average costs to equality."[34] Second, the survivor technique deals directly with plant size and hence circumvents the problem of allocating joint costs in multi-plant firms between those separate plants. Finally, the survivor technique deals with changes in the dynamic structure of industry, reflecting long-run trends and adjustments rather than the more normal static or comparative statics approach adopted for cost and production function estimates. Shepherd also identifies as a disadvantage of the technique an aspect which, so far as this present study is concerned, is a positive advantage. The survivor technique in addition to reflecting costs internal to the plant captures external costs and changes in external costs due to such factors as transportation costs, labor skills and the development of complementaries.

In view of earlier remarks regarding the assumption of perfect competition, the survivor technique is severely handicapped in the presence of strong monopoly elements, which raise problems of the appropriate definition of the industry and the market and hence of the product demand and the availability of imperfect substitutes. The optimal plant size cannot be specified without simultaneously specifying the product demand, and it is no longer possible to translate that surviving plant size range into a range of constant average total costs. From society's viewpoint, the firm's optimal plant size is sub-optimal.

The survivor technique, even when its implicit assumptions are satisfied, provides only descriptive estimates of optimality. These estimates may indicate the presence of scale economies by the survival of a particular range of plant sizes, but they do not provide an estimate of the degree, extent and significance of these economies.

Given the specific use of the survivor technique in this study to present supplementary evidence, other criticisms made by Shepherd are of minor consequence and hence are not discussed here.[35] However, Shepherd's cautionary note should be emphasized:

> "estimates need to be screened against other evidence
> . . . the survivor technique may, under favorable conditions yield preliminary or supplementary indications of certain ranges in the industry cost function . . .
> (but) application of the technique is unavoidably an art, not a purely objective, scientific process."[36]

In short, while the survivor estimates may be useful indicators and descriptors, they cannot be relied upon to provide primary evidence. Hence, survivor technique estimates are deferred to Chapter 10.

The necessary information to use these methods is available in the manuscripts of the federal censuses of manufacturing which are available to researchers for the nineteenth century. Unfortunately, the twentieth century documents are now protected by a court ruling on privacy. The data sources and problems with them are discussed below.

CHAPTER 3

THE DATA AND TESTS OF THE SAMPLES

I. <u>The Data</u>

The data underlying this study are drawn from the census manuscripts of manufactures for the census years 1850, 1860, and 1870,[1] and comprise two distinct sample groups. Collectively the samples will be referred to as the Bateman-Weiss sample. The procedures adopted by the Census Bureau have been described in detail by C. C. Wright[2] and are not repeated here.

The principal samples from the manuscript censuses comprise random samples of between 52 and 347 firms from each state for each census year. The published totals of the number of firms in each state were divided by the desired sample sizes to determine the number of firms, i, between each selected observation beginning with the pth firm, where p was a random number between one and i. These samples are supplemented by "large-firm" samples of the twenty largest firms by output in each state for each census year. Omissions from this schema are summarized in Table 3.1. Five 100 percent samples were taken and five samples were only partial due to the loss of the manuscripts. Records for Georgia and Louisiana have been destroyed and the manuscripts for twenty other samples for different states and years are currently unavailable.

The sample sizes and sampling proportions for those states which are currently available are shown in Table 3.2. Sampling proportions varied from a high of 1.16 for California in 1850, reflecting the serious omissions

Table 3.1

Peculiarities in, and Omissions from, the Sampling Procedure

Year and State	Peculiarity
I. 1850	
California	One hundred percent sample. Contains more firms than reported in the published census summary. See text.
Florida	One hundred percent sample. Contains more firms than reported in the published census summary. See text.
Georgia	Manuscripts destroyed.
Illinois	Manuscripts unavailable.
Kansas	Not constituted in 1850.
Louisiana	Manuscripts destroyed.
Michigan	Manuscripts available 1975.
Minnesota	Territory contained only five firms. Not sampled.
Oregon	One hundred percent sample. See text.
Rhode Island	Manuscripts unavailable.
Texas	One hundred percent sample. See text.
II. 1860	
Georgia	Manuscripts destroyed.
Louisiana	Manuscripts destroyed.
Michigan	Manuscripts available 1975.
Ohio	Partial sample due to the destruction of the manuscripts for 58 counties, including those for Cleveland, Cincinnati, Columbus, Dayton, and Toledo.
Oregon	One hundred percent sample. Contains fewer firms than reported in the census summary due to double counting. See text.

Table 3.1 (Continued)

Year and State	Peculiarity
Rhode Island	Manuscripts unavailable.
Tennessee	Partial sample due to the destruction of the manuscripts for 55 counties including those for Chatanooga, Knoxville, and Nashville.
III. 1870	
Delaware	Currently unavailable.
Georgia	Manuscripts destroyed.
Illinois	Partial sample, but includes Cook County. Records for 65 counties missing.
Indiana	Currently unavailable.
Iowa	Currently unavailable.
Louisiana	Manuscripts destroyed.
Maryland	Currently unavailable.
Michigan	Manuscripts available 1975.
Missouri	Currently unavailable.
Ohio	Partial sample. Records for 30 counties missing, but samples include Columbus, Cincinnati and Dayton.
Pennsylvania	Currently unavailable.
Rhode Island	Not included to the unavailability of the 1850 and 1860 manuscripts.
South Carolina	Currently unavailable.
Tennessee	Partial sample. Manuscripts for 57 counties missing including those for Knoxville and Memphis.
West Virginia	Not included.

Table 3.2

Sample Sizes and Sampling Proportions:
1850, 1860 and 1870

State	1850 Size	1850 Proportion	1860 Size	1860 Proportion	1870 Size	1870 Proportion
Alabama	237	.23	248	.17	275	.13
Arkansas	104	.40	112	.23	300	.28
California	93*	1.16	226	.16	192	.05
Connecticut	208	.06	199	.07	225	.05
Delaware	175	.33	183	.30	n.a.	n.a.
District of Columbia	139	.35	149	.36	185	.22
Florida	104*	1.02	77	.45	287	.46
Illinois	n.a.	n.a.	268	.06	132†	.01
Indiana	253	.06	295	.06	n.a.	n.a.
Iowa	178	.35	209	.11	n.a.	n.a.
Kansas	n.a.	n.a.	178	.85	n.a.	n.a.
Kentucky	310	.09	275	.08	221	.04
Maine	186	.05	168	.05	196	.04
Maryland	229	.06	223	.07	n.a.	n.a.
Massachusetts	190	.02	188	.03	187	.01
Minnesota	n.a.	n.a.	173	.31	179	.08
Mississippi	218	.23	243	.25	321	.19
Missouri	197	.07	190	.06	n.a.	n.a.
New Hampshire	200	.06	214	.08	193	.06
New Jersey	246	.06	237	.06	245	.04

Table 3.2 (Continued)

State	1850 Size	1850 Proportion	1860 Size	1860 Proportion	1870 Size	1870 Proportion
New York	233	.01	225	.01	162	.00
North Carolina	223	.09	219	.06	269	.07
Ohio	347	.03	101†	.01	180†	.01
Oregon	52	1.00	295††	.97	175	.18
Pennsylvania	262	.01	168	.01	n.a.	n.a.
South Carolina	285	.20	231	.19	n.a.	n.a.
Tennessee	236	.08	81†	.03	72†	.01
Texas	310*	1.02	262	.27	252	.11
Vermont	204	.11	219	.12	187	.06
Virginia	276	.06	271	.05	239	.04
Wisconsin	209	.17	201	.07	185	.03
Sum of the above	5,904	.05	6,328	.05	4,859	.02

*Errors and omissions in the published census summaries. See text.

†Partial sample of state due to destruction of manuscripts. See Table 3.1.

††Double counting by Census Bureau. Sample is actually greater than one hundred percent of the reported firms.

n.a. Not currently available.

from the published census which are discussed at length below, to a low of .0046 for New York state in 1870 which then was home to over 36,000 manufacturing establishments. Since the sample sizes bear no relation to the importance of manufacturing in each state relative to manufacturing in a region or the nation as a whole, one has to be careful about generalizing results at a more aggregated level. For this reason, as reported below, a variety of statistical tests were performed to establish the extent and degree of representativeness of these samples at varying levels of aggregation.

So far as the production function estimates reported here are concerned, the states were aggregated into regions as follows:

Region	States
Middle Atlantic	Delaware, the District of Columbia, Maryland, New Jersey, New York and Pennsylvania
New England	Connecticut, Maine, Massachusetts, New Hampshire and Vermont
Pacific	California and Oregon
Southern	Alabama, Arkansas, Florida, Kentucky, Mississippi, North Carolina, South Carolina, Tennessee, Texas and Virginia
Western	Illinois, Indiana, Iowa, Kansas, Minnesota, Missouri, Ohio and Wisconsin

and the production function estimates were made for each region and for the nation as a whole. The results of smaller subsets are given in my complete dissertation.

Of the nineteen items recorded in the manuscript censuses of manufactures for 1850 and 1860 and the twenty-one items recorded for 1870, this study makes explicit use of fourteen items for 1850 and 1860 and sixteen items in 1870.[3] The neglected items are essentially those unsuited to quantitative analysis.[4] Those items of record that were used are listed below with their variable names:

K = Capital invested, in real and personal estate, in the business

RQ = Quantities of raw materials used, including fuel

RV = Value of raw materials used, including fuel

PQ = Quantities of annual product

PV = Value of annual product

n_1 = Average number of male employees

n_2 = Average number of female employees

n_3 = Average number of youths employed (1870 only)

w_1 = Average monthly male wage bill

w_2 = Average monthly female wage bill

w_3 = Average monthly youth wage bill (1870 only)

M = Motive power source

HP = Horsepower

i = Firm subscript

j = Industry subscript

k = State subscript

C = City/township in which the establishment was located

The coding of the sample data collected by Bateman and Weiss provided for 104 distinct industry groupings. These were reduced to twelve, two-digit Standard Industrial Classification (SIC) codes:

Industry Group	SIC
Food and Kindred Products	20
Tobacco and Tobacco Products	21
Textile Mill Products	22
Apparel and Related Products	23
Lumber and Wood Products	24
Furniture and Fixtures	25
Chemicals and Allied Products	28
Leather and Leather Products	31
Primary Metals Products	33
Fabricated Metals Products	34
Non-electrical Machinery	35
Transportation Equipment	37

and estimates of the state, regional and national production functions for each of these SIC groups, as well as the aggregate (i.e., "all manufacturing") production function were made for each census year. These complete results are available in my complete dissertation, but for brevity and clarity of argument, we concentrate here upon the regional and national estimates. Indeed the principal focus will be even more narrowly defined by a subset of these namely the five largest industries, in terms of value-added, in 1850, 1860 and 1870. These were (alphabetically) boots and shoes, clothing, cotton textiles, flour milling and lumber milling. Although by 1870, the iron and steel industry exceeded, in terms of value-added, all others it has not been singled out because of the diversity in techniques between the furnace and the forge. Of these five industries, only boots and shoes, cottons and ready-made clothing were traded inter-regionally and therefore bear directly on the Russel-Linden-Genovese hypothesis. Flour and lumber were generally only locally traded. On the other hand, at least one firm in four was either a lumber mill or a flour mill and these represented the most typical manufacturing establishments.

II. Selection Criteria

Unfortunately not all data items were recorded for every firm by the census enumerators. It has therefore proved necessary to adopt some form of selection criteria to exclude those firms with missing data. The criteria adopted were not very exacting. Firms meeting one or more of the following conditions were excluded:

a) No labor input reported;

b) No wage data reported;

c) No capital reported;

d) No inputs or input values reported;

e) No outputs or output values reported;

f) Firm in an industry that was not considered to be a manufacturing activity (agricultural services such as threshing, builders, retail butchers, carpenters, cleaning, construction services such as painting, dentists, forestry, fishing, laundry, mining, photography, quarrying, repair services, salt works and transportation services);

g) Zero or negative value-added.

The final exclusion criterion had to be adopted due to the use of the logarithmic transformation. These criteria reduced the useable sample size to 5,565 firms in 1850, 6,076 firms in 1860 and 4,479 firms in 1870 by excluding 339 firms in 1850, 252 in 1860 and 380 in 1870.

III. Tests of the Samples

The purpose of reporting the sample tests in detail is fourfold. First, the data base of this study--the Bateman-Weiss samples--has not been described elsewhere and yet these data represent a significant advance in our ability to analyze systematically the progress of a long neglected sector of the developing American economy. Second, acceptance of the results of this study depend critically upon acceptance of the Bateman-Weiss samples as descriptors and adequate representatives of the parent populations: All manufacturing enterprises in the United States in 1850, 1860 and 1870. Third, an analysis of the samples, particularly the five 100 percent samples, provides some evidence upon the accuracy of the published census summaries. These latter sources have been used extensively by researchers with little regard to their accuracy and validity.[5] Such an analysis, therefore, permits us to reconstruct the decisions made by the Census Bureau compilers and at the same time to make some estimate of the magnitude of errors in the censuses. Finally, certain sample statistics such as mean output per establishment are used throughout the text in an attempt to explain the production function results and analyze their implications.

A. Accuracy of the Published Census

Tests of the samples rely upon the accuracy of the published census summaries. Unfortunately, the census summaries are frequently inaccurate and in a few cases contain gross inaccuracies and omissions. These shortcomings cannot be corrected, and consequently the sample tests must be interpreted as indicating the general state of the sample rather than an absolute judgment as to the worth and accuracy of any sample.

(a) The One Hundred Percent Samples

The collection of one hundred percent samples for California, Florida, Oregon and Texas in 1850 and Oregon in 1860 permit some inferences to be drawn with respect to the accuracy of the published census summaries and the decisions made by the Census Bureau in the allocation of firms between the various industry/product categories.

(i) California, 1850

Gross errors were found in the Census reporting for California in 1850. The census reports two flour mills producing an output valued at $754,192 while the manuscripts reveal that their output was only $77,950, a difference of $676,238. Further, the invested capital in flour milling is underreported by $15,000. Similarly, the Census Bureau failed to count eleven tin and sheet iron establishments employing 33 men and $57,700 capital and producing output valued at $514,280. The census also overstates the output of lumber mills by $70,400 and neglected to include one manufacturer of lemon syrup and one manufacturer of soda water. These offsetting errors make the California census summary appear more accurate than it is and the offsetting nature of these errors must therefore be kept in mind when interpreting the data in Table 3.3.

(ii) Florida, 1850

The Florida manuscripts contain 104 enterprises after the exclusion of logging operations (8 firms), fisheries (3 firms), salt refining (1 firm) and one firm of indeterminate industry. The published census summary indicates that Florida contained only 102 enterprises (104 firms are shown in Table 4 of the published summary, but this includes the salt refinery and an error in addition). Comparison between the sample and the published census reveals that five firms were counted twice by the Census Bureau. These five firms were saw-milling/flour milling conglomerates for which the Census Bureau arbitrarily divided the labor and capital between the

Table 3.3

A Comparison of One Hundred Per Cent Samples with the Published Census Results

	Number of Firms	Capital Invested	Cost of Raw Material	Employment	Annual Wage Bill	Value of Product
I. California, 1850						
Sample	93	340,825	881,645	418	837,780	3,629,785
Census	80	271,400	1,201,654	380	276,480	3,525,378
Difference	13	69,425	-320,009	38	561,300	104,407
Difference as a percentage of Census	16.25%	25.58%	-26.63%	10.0%	203.02%	2.96%
II. Florida, 1850						
Sample	104	825,260	220,263	1,290	251,880	708,295
Census	102[1]	528,060	220,611	983	198,948	662,335
Difference	2	297,200	-358	207	52,932	45,960
Difference as a percentage of Census	1.96%[1]	56.28%	-0.16%	21.06%	26.61%	6.94%
III. Oregon, 1850						
Sample	52	867,400	881,190	284	211,680	2,386,540
Census	52	843,600	809,560	285	388,620	2,236,640
Difference	0	23,800	71,630	-1	-176,940	149,900
Difference as a percentage of Census	0.00%	2.32%	8.85%	-0.35%	-45.53%	6.70%
IV. Oregon, 1860						
Sample	295	1,303,188	1,850,618	989	693,204	3,300,771
Census	304[2]	1,235,518	1,417,736	824	542,400	2,747,311
Difference	-9	67,670	432,882	165	150,804	553,460
Difference as a percentage of Census	-2.96%[2]	5.48%	30.53%	20.02%	27.80%	20.15%

Table 3.3
(Continued)

	Number of Firms	Capital Invested	Cost of Raw Material	Employment	Annual Wage Bill	Value of Product
V. Texas, 1850						
Sample	310	603,238	409,280	1,085	345,240	1,188,803
Census	307	535,840	392,892	1,050	320,016	1,162,438
Difference	3	67,398	16,388	35	25,224	26,365
Difference as a percentage of Census	0.98%	12.58%	4.17%	3.33%	2.27%	2.27%

[1] Correcting for double counting raises these figures to 7 and 7.22% respectively.

[2] Correcting for double counting raises these figures to 3 and 0.99% respectively.

Sources: Sample data from the Bateman-Weiss manuscript census samples.

two products, counting them both as lumber mills and as flour mills. Consequently according to the published summary, Florida should contain only 97 enterprises.

Nine legitimate enterprises contained within the sample, however, are not included in the published summary: four cotton presses with a combined capital investment of $89,000, employing 111 men and producing an output valued at $30,400 and five sugar refiners with a capital investment of $217,150 employing 121 men and 65 women and producing an output valued at $23,100. At the same time, the published summary shows two firms not included in the sample--a flour mill apparently producing $1,149 of output and a wheelright producing output valued at $3,300. Finally, the census under-reports the output of bakers by $1,500 while overstating the output of blacksmiths by $1,000.

(iii) Oregon, 1850

Interpretation of the Oregon 1850 manuscripts proved difficult due to numerous corrections obscuring and confusing the figures and the (apparent) pricing of planking in Clackamas County in dollars per thousand feet. However, it appears that (arithmetic) errors led to an overstatement of capital invested in lumber milling by $13,000, and employment by 1, while understating the cost of raw materials by $56,640 and output by $28,800. The Census Bureau further understated the cost of raw materials by $14,990 and the value of output by $121,100 for flour milling, thereby compounding the errors made in lumber milling, while offsetting some of their error in capital invested by understating it by $36,800.

(iv) Oregon, 1860

The 1860 Oregon census summary proved to be no better than that for 1850. Arithmetic errors abound in almost every category and the Census Bureau persisted in double counting flour mill/lumber mill conglomerates, consequently immediately overstating the number of individual establishments by five. The manufacture of saddle trees is overstated by one hundred percent due to the same firm being included on two separate pages of the manuscripts. A Blacksmith who indicated that he also repaired wagons was also double counted. The manuscripts also reveal two fewer boot and shoe manufacturers than counted by the census. Indeed, errors exist in at least seventeen of twenty-seven product categories listed by the Census. As with the 1850 censuses not only were double counting and arithmetic errors serious problems but also the omission from the published census of legitimate enterprises further confuses the issue. Five firms were apparently omitted from the 1860 Oregon Census summary: one meat packer, one planing mill, one gas manufacturer, one shipyard and one manufacturer of beehives.

(v) Texas, 1850

According to the published census, Texas in 1850 supported 89 sawmills, yet the census manuscripts reveal only 65 lumber mills and 15 lumber milling/flour milling conglomerates. Even neglecting the possible arbitrary division of labor and capital between the two pursuits, the published census apparently overstates the value of lumber by $98,985. But this discrepancy is more than offset by the Census Bureau's miscalculations for flour milling. The manuscripts contain 17 flour mills, plus the fifteen flour mill/lumber mills already noted, yet the Census reports only 14. Output of flour is

understated by $52,704 or by more than one hundred percent of the reported
value. Indeed, census errors for Texas in 1850 are too numerous to list.
Many of these errors are minor arithmetic errors, but some (as noted above)
represent gross errors. Finally, the census summary omits one confectioner,
four cotton gin manufacturers, two cotton presses and five meat packers, so
that the one hundred percent Texas sample contains six firms more than shown
by the census.

(b) The Samples as a Whole

Clearly, therefore, extreme caution must be exercised when interpreting
the sample tests. Failure to satisfy the test cannot be taken as an absolute judgment against the sample, nor can any satisfactory correction be
made to the census summaries to improve their accuracy. In some cases,
census errors cancel out while in others they compound themselves. Indeed,
it is probable that the samples themselves provide a better description of
the parent population than the published census summaries.

Although no one hundred percent samples were taken for any state in
1870, it is unlikely that the number and seriousness of errors in the
published census is less than was found for 1850 or 1860. Indeed, a number
of errors and omissions are apparent just from the samples. For example
in Florida, the published census reports only three leather tanners with a
combined capital investment of $8,000, employing eleven men and producing
an output value at $13,800. However, the Census failed to count at least
one other leather tanner, with a capital of $1,200, employing three men
and producing $2,800 of output. In Mississippi, the census summary reports
four railroad repairing and rail car manufactures with a capital investment

of $212,500, employing two hundred and twenty-one men and producing output valued at $284,631. The sample for Mississippi contains three such operations, two being owned by the Southern Railroad and one owned by the V and M Railroad. Together these operations employed $126,000 capital and 197 men to produce an output valued at $279,441. Since each of these figures from the sample is less than the corresponding estimate from the published census, the census estimate is still possible. However, the implied statistics for the fourth firm are not plausible since they imply that $86,500 capital and twenty-four men produced an output valued at only $5,190. Moreover, if the data are broken down into rail cars and railroad repairing, we find that while the Census estimate for rail cars shows employment of 111 men and $122,500 capital producing output valued at $143,401, the sample shows that employment was actually only 91 men, and that their output was actually $40 greater. The differences between the census and the sample data are small but they do point to the possibility of much larger errors in more populous and complex industry categories.

B. Representativeness of the Samples

As noted in Tables 3.1 and 3.2 a number of samples in 1870 were only partial samples due to the loss or destruction of the manuscripts. For example, thirty counties are missing from the Ohio manuscripts, fifteen of them among the 58 counties which were missing for 1860. The missing data in 1870, however, are less serious than for 1860, since the 1870 data include Cincinnati, Cleveland, and Columbus. Similarly, data were missing for parts of Tennessee in 1860 and 1870. This loss is more serious since the data for both Knoxville and Memphis are missing from the 1870 Tennessee sample and may result in a serious bias in the Tennessee results. Data for sixty-five Illinois counties are also missing from the 1870 manuscripts, but fortunately Cook county is not one of those missing.

Two tests of the samples were made. These tests provide some indication about the relative merits of each sample and serve to illuminate possible problem areas vis a vis the population where significant differences between the sample statistics and the population parameters could not be resolved by a careful rechecking of the samples.

(a) Distribution of Firms by Industry

Given the random sampling schema, the industrial distribution of firms within each state from the samples should approximate that of the parent population. A chi-square test for goodness of fit was therefore performed on each state sample for each year. Using the sample proportions given in Table 3.2 and data from the published census summaries of the industrial distribution of firms by state, the expected number of firms in each industry for each state, E_i, was calculated and compared with the observed number of firms in that industry in the state, O_i. The statistic

$$\sum_{i=1}^{n} \frac{(O_i - E_i)^2}{E_i}$$

then follows the chi-square distribution with (n-1) degrees of freedom.

Table 3.4 reports these chi-square results. Many chi-square values were significant at the five percent level indicating that the industrial distribution of firms in those samples were significantly different to that derived from the published census summaries. In almost every case

Table 3.4

Goodness of Fit and the Industrial Distribution of Firms
Chi-Square Values

State	Unadjusted 1850	1860	1870	Adjusted 1850	1860	1870
Alabama	54.31*	17.41	39.03*	38.36*	15.37	2.96
Arkansas	54.63*	10.74	3627.83*	6.37	9.31	35.45*
California	50.59*	12.44	42.45*	49.94*[1]	10.74	42.33*
Connecticut	33.69*	13.00	17.55	29.69*	10.51	17.26
Delaware	17.96	21.48	n.a.	15.47	16.54	n.a.
District of Columbia	13.96	11.77	14.02	10.53	9.11	12.78
Florida	81.33*	8.58	372.99*	81.17*[2]	6.86	20.20
Illinois	n.a.	13.34	14.05	n.a.	12.84	13.36
Indiana	19.01	14.35	n.a.	11.19	7.95	n.a.
Iowa	15.23	8.75	n.a.	14.68	6.77	n.a.
Kansas	n.a.	3.10	n.a.	n.a.	2.76	n.a.
Kentucky	28.73*	68.28*	28.96*	14.13	15.26	11.16[6]
Maine	51.81*	11.84	20.33	12.93	10.31	20.60
Maryland	94.29*	333.15*	n.a.	9.66	14.31	n.a.
Massachusetts	17.35	495.00*	17.38	14.42	14.69	15.31
Minnesota	n.a.	50.13*	23.77*	n.a.	7.22	17.91
Mississippi	15.90	12.76	4491.42*	13.41	6.66	18.64[6]
Missouri	19.83	17.45	n.a.	18.36	15.80	n.a.
New Hampshire	17.39	151.21*	17.40	13.02	10.22	16.70
New Jersey	24.91*	60.16*	8.87	24.66*	12.55	8.66
New York	421.63*	104.32*	9.84	22.22	15.06	8.35
North Carolina	10.22	52.45*	51.07*	9.02*	51.79*	13.65
Ohio	49.64*	11.04	20.08	13.11	10.43*	13.58

Table 3.4 (Continued)

State	Unadjusted 1850	1860	1870	Adjusted 1850	1860	1870
Oregon	0.00	12.12	133.24*	0.00	4.24	132.15*
Pennsylvania	367.18*	34.81*	n.a.	16.69	20.53*	n.a.
South Carolina	13.37	11.69	n.a.	12.78	9.51	n.a.
Tennessee	528.46*	10.56	424.40*	14.21	9.66	11.90
Texas	15.71	4.59	344.32*	11.22	2.33	12.40
Vermont	8.90	16.52	25.03*	6.47	16.39	24.11*
Virginia	114.20*	24.76*	11.99	113.77*[3]	17.81	11.69
West Virginia	n.a.	n.a.	n.a.	n.a.	n.a.	n.a.
Wisconsin	36.95*	10.63	6.90	10.71	8.65	6.73

[1] Census contains gross omissions of tin-smithing. Excluding tin-smithing reduces the chi-square value to 0.93.

[2] If the Census is corrected for the omission of the nine firms, the corrected chi-square falls to 2.07.

[3] Census contains gross omissions of lumber milling. Excluding lumber from the distribution lowers the chi-square to 28.86 (significant at the 5% level).

[4] Census apparently underreported lumber milling while including gatherers of crude turpentine. Excluding these two categories reduces the chi-square to 9.4.

[5] With Agricultural Implements (140 industry groups) included in Black-smithing.

[6] With Iron Manufacture (120), Machinery (150) and Transportation Equipment (230) aggregated.

*Indicates that the industrial distribution of firms within the sample differed significantly from the distribution given in the published census summaries.

three industry categories, blacksmithing, wagon and carriage making and meat packing, accounted for these differences in 1850 and 1860.

A careful review of the manuscripts reveals that many blacksmiths also made wagons, while many carriage makers also did repair work. The distinction between blacksmiths and wagon and carriage makers is therefore very blurred. Similarly, for meat packing it proved very difficult to distinguish between slaughter-houses catering to the retail trade and meat packers. Consequently, for the purposes of these tests, blacksmithing, carriage and wagon makers and meat packing were excluded. The adjusted chi-square values with these three industry groups excluded in 1850 and 1860 are also reported in Table 3.4.

The unadjusted chi-square statistics for 1870 given in Table 3.4 show many samples to have significantly different industrial distributions of firms from those given in the published census. Twelve of the twenty-three results indicated significant differences at the five percent level, eight of these being Southern states. For the South, the significance of the chi-square statistic is largely accounted for by the omission from the Census of Manufactures of the cotton ginning. The adjusted chi-square statistics reported in Table 3.4 therefore exclude this industry category. However, many results remained significant and no single criterion such as was used for 1850 and 1860 seemed possible. For Kentucky and Mississippi, iron manufacture, machinery and railroad equipment were combined into a single industry category, while in Alabama, agricultural implement manufacturers were included with Blacksmiths. No other plausible adjustments or minor reassignments between industrial groups for the remaining states would reduce the value of the chi-square statistic to a non-significant level.

The adjustments reduced the number of samples with industrial distributions significantly different to those derived from the published census from 37 to 14. Moreover, for California 1850, Florida 1850 and North Carolina 1860, known errors in the published census summaries account for these significant differences. The census omitted eleven tin-smiths from the published statistics for California 1850, and four cotton presses and five sugar refiners from Florida 1850. A careful study of the North Carolina 1860 manuscripts reveals the exclusion of many legitimate lumber mills while including gatherers of crude turpentine. Making additional adjustments for these errors reduces the chi-square values to levels that are not significantly different from zero. The Virginia 1850 chi-square statistic similarly benefits from the exclusion of lumber milling. The published census summary for Virginia 1850 reports only two lumber mills in the state, yet the sample contains sixteen lumber mills and eighteen lumber mill/flour mill conglomerates implying that the state must have contained at least 266 lumber mills. Making this correction dramatically reduces the value of the chi-square statistic, though it remains significantly different to zero due to the (apparent) under-representation of flour mills in the sample.

Problems with the 1870 statistics are amply illustrated by the results for Oregon. The 1870 Oregon sample on the basis of the published statistics contains too few lumber mills, iron and tinware manufacturers, and boot and shoe and textile establishments, while at the same time containing too many carriage and wagon manufacturers and flour mills. Almost every industry category is affected. Whether or not the published census is in error is not known at the present time, but in view of earlier findings from the one hundred percent samples, the probability of census error is fairly high.

(b) t-tests on Firm Statistics

On the basis of the random sampling criterion one would expect that the samples would have statistics similar to those of the parent population. Four statistics are of special interest:

    i) Output per establishment;

    ii) Output/Labor ratio;

    iii) Output/Input ratio;

and iv) Capital/Labor ratio;

each of which is directly or indirectly related to the variables used in the estimation of the production functions.

The correspondence between these sample statistics and those of the parent population was checked using the t-test,

$$t = \frac{\bar{x} - \mu}{s/\sqrt{n}} .$$

The aggregate results by state and year are reported in Tables 3.5 - 3.7. Unfortunately, due to the errors and omissions in the published census summaries, these tests once again cannot be treated as definitive indicators of the proximity of the sample statistics to those of the population. Indeed, they are probably more descriptive of the true population values than those derived directly from the published census.

In almost every case, however, the Output/Input ratio proved to be significantly greater than that for the parent population. Results from the one hundred percent samples indicate that where both the cost of raw materials and the value of the output was underreported by the Census, the underreporting of output values was always numerically greater than the underreporting of raw material costs, while for Florida 1850 and California 1850, the Census overreports the cost of raw materials while underreporting the value of output. Both types of error would have the effect of raising the population estimates of the Output/Input ratio.

However, aggregated results may be misleading. Out of four hundred and twenty t-tests on the Output/Input ratio for 1850, only fifteen were significantly different from the industry population values for the ninety-five percent confidence interval. Given the level of significance chosen one would have expected as many as twenty-one to be significantly different from the population values.

On the other hand, the apparent accuracy of the sample estimates of output per establishment shown in Table 3.5 is not supported at the industry level. Fifty-nine of the t-tests showed a significant difference (at the five percent level), between the sample estimates and those for the population, and fifty-six of these indicated that the sample estimates were less than those for the population.

For large samples, the t-distribution approximates the normal distribution and, hence, one would expect that the computed t-ratios would be normally distributed. Taking this to be the null hypothesis versus the alternative hypothesis that the t-ratios are not normally distributed, a chi-square test for goodness of fit was performed. The null hypothesis is not rejected for only fourteen of the forty-five distributions examined, eight of which are for output per establishment, and none for the output/input ratio.

Table 3.5

AGGREGATE MEAN VALUES OF SAMPLE STATISTICS
1850
(Standard Error)

State	Output per Establishment ($)	Output/Labor Ratio ($ per employee)	Output/Input Ratio	Capital/Labor Ratio ($ per employee)
Alabama	4558.15 (664.34)	1016.18 (118.22)	4.56* (.56)	617.19 (59.00)
Arkansas	2311.69 (353.42)	899.55 (150.96)	3.80* (.15)	404.19 (60.07)
California	39323.97 (5912.73)	9354.49 (1160.47)	5.41* (.88)	725.24 (161.15)
Connecticut	11810.50 (1886.81)	1269.85* (149.12)	2.62* (.23)	523.71 (48.52)
Delaware	8604.68 (2443.71)	1360.87 (186.63)	2.85* (.29)	703.20 (92.14)
District of Columbia	5152.86 (978.44)	1280.56 (212.35)	2.77* (.41)	388.40 (61.16)
Florida	6810.53 (1323.02)	666.16 (83.20)	5.03* (.71)	576.50 (69.99)
Indiana	4791.58 (838.64)	1400.56 (207.52)	3.67* (.38)	545.10 (54.21)
Iowa	6142.37 (985.87)	1552.32** (198.33)	3.45* (.44)	790.79 (103.67)
Kentucky	8747.12 (1857.71)	979.03 (89.81)	3.78* (.39)	609.46 (84.09)
Maine	6307.52 (1464.81)	839.95 (79.79)	2.91* (.26)	443.41 (47.28)
Maryland	7420.50 (1000.92)	1515.64* (186.16)	2.66* (.23)	535.55 (75.23)
Massachusetts	20891.54 (4196.11)	1449.70* (187.55)	3.02* (.32)	524.98 (59.64)
Mississippi	4263.02 (1200.49)	865.34 (118.64)	13.72 (9.40)	513.05 (57.55)

Table 3.5 (cont.)

State	Output per Establishment	Output/Labor Ratio	Output/Input Ratio	Capital/Labor Ratio
Missouri	6888.06 (1320.12)	1342.86 (155.26)	3.76* (.38)	435.55 (71.72)
New Hampshire	7037.19 (1040.09)	1325.31* (151.47)	2.55* (.25)	550.65** (60.52)
New Jersey	8534.32 (1331.86)	1703.58* (195.71)	3.17* (.68)	1025.23* (122.12)
New York	11112.19 (2576.51)	1604.03 (209.64)	2.96* (.25)	727.35* (80.38)
North Caarolina	2955.30 (440.38)	911.67* (107.89)	2.94* (.41)	653.85* (65.44)
Ohio	5300.88 (773.62)	1282.28 (114.88)	3.67* (.33)	629.93 (57.46)
Oregon	45895.00 (8417.50)	12856.99 (2763.44)	5.43* (1.09)	3686.26 (1065.10)
Pennsylvania	9946.01 (1969.44)	1580.18* (162.87)	2.49* (.19)	922.52* (100.80)
South Carolina	4108.08 (703.14)	1034.83 (120.57)	4.51* (.81)	746.36 (74.81)
Tennessee	4770.65 (976.02)	946.37 (85.92)	3.78* (.43)	498.14 (48.72)
Texas	3755.45 (364.83)	1056.28 (76.34)	4.88* (.41)	548.05 (65.89)
Vermont	4440.23 (751.70)	1106.91 (116.23)	3.19* (.30)	625.15 (65.03)
Virginia	6072.24 (1012.59)	1436.09 (150.26)	2.52* (.22)	846.24* (109.05)
Wisconsin	7924.46 (1224.19)	1975.77 (312.96)	3.29* (.32)	661.98 (75.41)

Footnotes: *Sample statistic significantly greater (at the five percent level) than the population parameter.

**Sample statistic significantly less (at the five percent level) than the population parameter.

An attractive alternative null hypothesis, that errors were uniformly distributed about the true values was also tested. This null hypothesis is accepted for only thirteen of the forty-five distributions, a performance marginally worse than the hypothesis of a normal distribution. Indeed, if one accepts the sample estimates as accurate, then the published census summaries appear to be consistent in only one respect; their inaccuracy.

Essentially similar, though marginally poorer results at the state level were obtained for 1860. These results are shown in Table 3.6. At the state level all sample estimates of the Output/Input ratio were significantly different from the corresponding population values, although at the industry level only fourteen of four hundred and sixty-five t-tests on this statistic were significantly different from those of the population. In each case, the sample estimate was greater than the population value.

At the state level, where output per establishment differed from the population value, the sample estimate was lower. At the same time the output/labor ratio was generally larger than for the population. At the industry level, seventy-seven estimates of output per establishment were significantly different from the published census estimates, all but one of them indicating smaller mean firm sizes in the samples than in the parent population. Twenty-seven of the industry output/labor ratios also proved significant.

The hypothesis that the t-ratios are normally distributed is not rejected for only eleven of the forty-five distributions tested, suggesting that the distribution of errors in the samples vis a vis the population is not normal. A similar result was obtained for 1850. Overall, as noted

Table 3.6

AGGREGATE MEAN VALUES OF SAMPLE STATISTICS
1860
(Standard Error)

State	Output per Establishment	Output/Labor Ratio	Output/Input Ratio	Capital/Labor Ratio
Alabama	7720.85 (1405.61)	1733.11 (206.14)	3.37* (.28)	871.56** (82.16)
Arkansas	6723.79 (1056.69)	1987.79 (344.75)	4.15* (.57)	689.21 (96.79)
California	12033.38** (1665.03)	3067.34 (345.18)	4.68* (.69)	1109.63** (120.64)
Connecticut	25795.73 (4354.53)	1847.07* (217.90)	3.15* (.44)	823.51 (90.61)
Delaware	19547.79 (4485.97)	2013.96 (257.07)	2.76* (.28)	991.55 (136.19)
District of Columbia	11409.97 (2286.72)	2646.05 (540.39)	4.92* (1.42)	732.80 (119.86)
Florida	14502.22 (3522.06)	1229.28 (194.02)	4.33* (.67)	761.75 (110.86)
Illinois	9812.83** (1303.09)	2176.04 (229.39)	3.21* (.33)	1080.17 (113.32)
Indiana	7557.49 (911.89)	2240.97 (253.11)	3.16* (.26)	1024.05 (102.89)
Iowa	5834.91 (790.85)	2100.34 (286.92)	2.94* (.28)	1148.55 (119.45)
Kansas	12852.95 (1937.77)	2360.31** (272.09)	6.37* (1.01)	924.07 (189.58)
Kentucky	10223.01 (1430.43)	2308.50 (244.02)	2.64* (.21)	884.31 (99.16)
Maine	14261.38 (4084.91)	1511.28 (416.86)	3.42* (.39)	566.27 (68.12)
Maryland	19744.23 (4083.25)	2775.16* (386.13)	2.88* (.27)	944.91 (121.44)
Massachusetts	32558.00 (5776.50)	2463.08* (398.92)	3.08* (.39)	779.42 (92.51)
Minnesota	5239.29 (859.59)	1733.76 (215.68)	2.86* (.27)	1325.46 (329.97)

Table 3.6 (cont.)

State	Output per Establishment	Output/Labor Ratio	Output/Input Ratio	Capital/Labor Ratio
Mississippi	6889.88 (1018.03)	1484.38 (169.05)	3.70* (.33)	838.67 (90.32)
Missouri	16338.34 (4972.18)	1799.85 (215.71)	4.56* (.80)	906.05 (135.32)
New Hampshire	8562.42** (1908.68)	1582.84 (267.40)	2.91* (.30)	702.86 (76.27)
New Jersey	27534.12 (4979.77)	2179.30* (256.09)	3.16* (.33)	1125.64* (142.99)
New York	16739.03 (4220.71)	1967.36 (239.08)	2.79* (.24)	889.05 (96.91)
North Carolina	4686.24 (550.28)	2088.12* (246.02)	2.78* (.23)	881.89* (92.45)
Ohio	9752.48 (2881.39)	1973.23 (453.85)	3.21* (.41)	797.08 (125.06)
Oregon	10739.06 (1485.57)	4314.06 (521.04)	6.02* (.83)	1742.27 (166.77)
Pennsylvania	10092.39 (1787.86)	2024.03* (252.86)	2.80* (.33)	1110.14 (143.92)
South Carolina	8419.78 (1587.40)	1600.18 (183.51)	3.04* (.30)	935.68 (91.61)
Tennessee	11051.63 (2866.52)	2411.94* (462.00)	4.02* (.97)	991.19 (173.95)
Texas	8859.29 (1286.12)	2580.29 (347.43)	11.75 (6.70)	397.53 (85.14)
Vermont	7456.57 (1687.10)	1595.02 (185.83)	3.53* (.64)	907.56 (124.75)
Virginia	13798.56 (2649.34)	2364.20* (276.29)	2.70* (.22)	1113.92* (118.80)
Wisconsin	9081.42 (1482.41)	2126.66 (318.70)	3.08* (.29)	1025.08 (124.73)

Footnotes: See Table 3.5.

earlier, the 1860 results are marginally worse than those for 1850, probably reflecting the increasing complexity of the American industrial system and the failure of census methods to keep pace. For example, whereas the 1850 census had identified only 262 separate products, by 1860, 631 separate products were listed, a two hundred and forty percent increase in ten years.

Student's t-test statistics for 1870, given in Table 3.7, reflect this worsening trend. At the state level only three of the twenty-three sample estimates of output per establishment differed significantly from those given in the published census, while six of the output/labor ratios and seven of the capital-labor ratios were significantly different.

The method of presentation of summary statistics adopted by the Census Bureau in 1870 made compilation of accurate industry statistics difficult. For example, the Census Bureau chose to report statistics of agricultural implement manufacturers separately under the heading of "Special Statistics for Manufactures", while Boot and Shoe manufactures among others, are reported in both the general and the special tables. The Census Bureau also compiled some industry group estimates such as lumber, including lumber planed and sawed, and staves, shooks and headings not all of which were separately reported, while lumber was also included in the Building Materials category as well as being separately reported.

As before, at the industry level the sample estimates of the output/input ratio proved to be one of the best statistics despite its dismal failure at the state level. Only fourteen of the two hundred and ninty-six estimates were significantly different from the population values, as

Table 3.7

AGGREGATE MEAN VALUES OF SAMPLE STATISTICS
1870
(Standard Error)

State	Output per Establishment	Output/Labor Ratio	Output/Input Ratio	Capital/Labor Ratio
Alabama	6843.88 (1070.25)	3598.76* (750.01)	3.90* (.45)	740.88 (77.94)
Arkansas	5563.25* (535.98)	1738.45 (149.11)	2.97* (.25)	473.89 (48.99)
California	10968.21** (1558.87)	2072.66** (255.79)	3.57* (.34)	903.64** (113.13)
Connecticut	38852.62 (7014.29)	2345.39 (295.25)	2.99* (.28)	1259.61 (194.90)
District of Columbia	6531.79** (1019.47)	1724.86 (171.10)	4.09* (.40)	612.12** (84.76)
Florida	7196.00 (1080.97)	1767.91 (163.64)	3.08* (.42)	382.68** (30.94)
Illinois	25208.03 (9612.54)	2360.09 (492.78)	3.72* (.49)	1028.53 (193.36)
Kentucky	14824.23 (3203.33)	1879.44 (207.34)	3.14* (.26)	763.05** (95.95)
Maine	20975.49 (5049.48)	1741.54 (264.32)	2.96* (.28)	820.47 (117.13)
Massachusetts	40964.84 (7970.58)	2201.48 (248.93)	4.19* (.58)	787.76 (106.04)
Minnesota	7963.98 (1391.90)	2044.39 (324.48)	3.27* (.37)	943.93 (108.36)
Mississippi	5457.24 (644.66)	2114.46* (242.26)	2.99* (.33)	599.80** (55.54)
Mew Hampshire	42010.10 (24068.46)	2122.25 (311.30)	3.08* (.31)	909.05 (116.55)
New Jersey	30819.09 (8640.63)	3407.18* (439.91)	3.26* (.31)	1388.65 (179.86)

Table 3.7 (cont.)

State	Output per Establishment	Output/Labor Ratio	Output/Input Ratio	Capital/Labor Ratio
New York	25766.04 (6399.87)	2868.70 (453.47)	3.84* (.55)	1554.25 (511.31)
North Carolina	5054.99 (713.68)	1960.54* (241.89)	2.36* (.21)	757.27* (7.08)
Ohio	19529.11 (7190.81)	2467.97 (445.27)	3.10* (.36)	908.06 (128.55)
Oregon	7460.50 (1999.50)	2479.77 (382.09)	3.75* (.34)	1313.34 (154.78)
Tennessee	6152.83 (1781.89)	1976.20 (413.09)	2.75* (.50)	883.96 (338.44)
Texas	6178.75 (919.09)	1791.68 (191.64)	2.83* (.27)	721.68 (107.77)
Vermont	15467.71 (8341.11)	1754.49 (228.01)	3.69* (.38)	867.61** (91.76)
Virginia	5736.42 (1505.08)	2230.67* (394.95)	3.64* (.59)	770.72 (97.55)
Wisconsin	10878.82 (3048.77)	1751.55 (273.29)	3.18* (.32)	1084.18 (209.01)

Footnotes: See Table 3.5.

compared with twenty-three of the output/labor ratios and sixty-eight of the output per establishment estimates.

In 1870, the Census Bureau only identified 392 separate products, down from the 631 products identified in 1860. It is possible that the combination of separate products under a single product heading may have resulted in more numerous omissions from the 1870 Census. Testing of such a hypothesis must, however, await the collection of some one hundred percent samples for 1870. Certainly, since errors in the published summary are apparent just from the regular Bateman-Weiss samples, it appears likely that errors in 1870 will exceed those for 1850 and 1860.

IV. Other Variables

Although the census manuscripts and the Bateman-Weiss samples contain most of the necessary basic information from which make the production function estimates, some of this data is inadequate or in a less desirable form given the use to which it will be put.

A. Capital

The capital estimates reported in the censuses are generally accepted as representing the gross book value of invested capital at the original cost.[6] Such estimates are far removed from the required capital services variable and they present grave conceptual problems. Indeed, Superintendant of the Census repeatedly argued that:

> "The data compiled in respect to capital . . . have been so defective as to be of little value except as indicating general conditions. In fact it has been repeatedly recommended by the census authorities that this inquiry be omitted from the schedule"[7]

This inquiry was dropped after 1920. On the nineteenth century capital estimates the Superintendant of the Census wrote:

> "The form of the inquiry regarding capital at all censuses down to and including 1880 was so vague and general in its character that it cannot be assumed that any true proportion exists between the statistics on this subject as elicited prior to 1890"[8]

Despite these serious defects, the absence of better estimates has compelled the use of the census capital figures. But an attempt has been made to correct these data for some of the potential sources of bias.

Since the Census inquiry apparently excluded working capital which also contributes services to the production process, reported invested capital has been adjusted to take account of this exclusion. Working capital is represented by trade credit, stocks of raw materials on hand and goods in process or inventory. It is thus largely dependent upon the level of output and upon the type of industry and its geographic location.

Adjustment was based upon the rates of "live assets"/PV taken from the 1890 published census.[9] These parameters are summarized in Table 3.8 and appear to satisfy the criteria. One peculiarity emerges from these data. Fogel[10] argued that working capital varied inversely with the level of development as speedier and more certain transportation reduced optimum inventory levels and the volume of goods in transit. This is doubtless true, but the need for working capital appears to have increased, not decreased as the extension of trade credit becomes a cost of doing business replacing the cash basis adopted in the less commercially developed areas.

Table 3.8

Mean Parameters for Twelve Selected Industry Groups
from the 1890 Census by Region

Region	"Live Assets"/ Output (ρ)	Buildings/ Capital (b)	Machinery/ Capital (m)	Miscellaneous Expenses/ Capital (irm)	Officers/ Employees (s)
The Middle States[1]	.379	.327	.365	.241	.173
The New England States[2]	.415	.331	.458	.623	.141
The Pacific States[3]	.443	.212	.490	.544	.171
The Southern States[4]	.290	.274	.479	.531	.180
The Western States[5]	.373	.332	.377	.318	.170

Footnotes: [1]Delaware, District of Columbia, Maryland, New Jersey, New York, and Pennsylvania.

[2]Connecticut, Maine, Massachusetts, New Hampshire and Vermont.

[3]California and Oregon.

[4]Alabama, Arkansas, Florida, Kentucky, Mississippi, North Carolina, South Carolina, Tennessee, Texas and Virginia.

[5]Illinois, Indiana, Iowa, Kansas, Minnesota, Missouri, Ohio, and Wisconsin.

The resultant capital estimate:

$$K_i^* = K_i + \rho_{jk} \cdot PV_i$$

where ρ is the appropriate industry and state parameter. This remains, however, a stock rather than a flow variable.

The 1890 Census[11] also contains information on insurance, maintenance and repairs together with a breakdown of invested capital into land, buildings and machinery. This information may be used to approximate a capital services variable. These services should depend upon the stock reported by the Census and upon its composition. The breakdown of invested capital into buildings and machinery provided estimates of the fraction of invested capital in each at earlier dates by industry and state. I assumed that this composition did not change. The averages of these, by region, are shown in Table 3.8.

Depreciation was estimated by assuming an expected life-span of 50 years for buildings and 15 years for machinery.[12] The straightline method was used and depreciation was estimated by the fraction:

$$d_{jk} = \{(b_{jk}/50) + (m_{jk}/15)\}$$

Likewise estimates for insurance, maintenance and repairs were derived from the 1890 ratio of miscellaneous expenses/invested capital. Together these provide for the perpetuation of the capital and measure, at least partially, the services contributed by capital to the production process. Thus the capital services variable is defined by:

$$K_i^{**} = (d_{jk} + irm_{jk}) \cdot K_i + r \cdot K_i^*$$

where r is the rate of interest (assumed to be six percent).

This method, albeit imperfect, does embody the essence of the notion of a service flow but to the extent that it requires greater expressions of faith in the assumption of ceteris paribus between 1850, 1860 or 1870 and 1890 it is to be less preferred than the capital stock measure, K_i^*. In some recent research, Griliches had access to both kinds of measures of capital for production functions and concluded that the capital stock measure gave similar, though marginally inferior, results to those obtained using the capital services measure.[13] Use of the latter is therefore confined to the chapter on sensitivity analysis.[14]

B. Labor

Measurement of labor presents two problems. First is the problem of reporting accuracy by the census. The inquiry regarding labor was unclear with respect to the inclusion of the proprietor or salaried managers. From a study of the manuscripts one must conclude that such personnel were almost certainly excluded. For small firms the exclusion of the proprietor represents a significant understatement of the labor input.

Recourse has been made again to the published 1890 census. Parameters have been derived for the ratio of salaried personnel/employees (see Table 3.8) and these may be used as a basis for adjusting the labor input. This managerial labor was valued at twice the adult employee equivalent.

Second, the labor input, like the capital input, should be measured in terms of a flow rather than a stock, that is in terms of man-hours of labor equivalent, rather than in terms of number of employees. However there exist no statistics on man-hours for this period and furthermore most industries were seasonal. For example, as late as 1890, flour mills operated an average of only seven months a year, while least season-dependent industries such as agricultural implement averaged ten months and wagons and carriages only eleven.[15] Seasonality about the middle of the nineteenth century was undoubtedly more pronounced due to the greater dependence upon waterpower and the poorer communications system.

Moreover, expression of the labor input in man-hour equivalents presupposes knowledge of the appropriate weights for managerial, for skilled, for unskilled and for female and juvenile labor. To the extent that wages were observed (for males, females and in some cases, for juveniles), employees could be weighted by their wage rate relative to the male wage rate. This would be a correct weighing scheme only if the degree of exploitation across classes of labor was constant. Of course, though, if exploitation existed, in the sense of labor receiving less than the value of its marginal product, then the sum would still be incorrect.

Consequently, reliance has been placed upon the simple unweighted sum of employees as reported in the census:

$$L = n_1 + n_2 + n_3$$

and an appeal to the results of the sensitivity analysis performed in Chapter 7.

Despite the potential downward bias in the labor input due to the exclusion of the proprietors and managers, it is probable that this bias is more than offset by the assumption that labor is employed full-time on a twelve month basis. This upward bias to the labor input necessarily imparts a downward bias upon the economies of scale parameter. While in the _ex ante_ production model the optimal quantities of labor and capital are jointly determined, in the _ex post_ model labor and capital are to a limited degree independent of one another since in the short-run only labor is variable. Consequently an upward bias in the labor input necessarily implies a downward bias in the sum of coefficients. Moreover, the greater the degree of independence between labor and capital the greater will be the degree of downward bias upon labor coefficient, the output elasticity with respect to labor, relative to the capital coefficient.

C. The Measurement of Output

While data on the physical quantities of inputs and output are given in the census manuscripts, they are generally felt to be unreliable. This lack of reliability stems from the rudimentary nature of nineteenth century weights and measures, together with haphazard reporting by the census enumerators. For example, according to the 1828 edition of Webster's Dictionary, a barrel of flour in New York State weighed anywhere between 196 and 228 pounds, a variation too great to be accounted for by variations in moisture content alone. Thus, it is not surprising that prices of even fairly homogeneous commodities such as wheat flour varied widely within and between states.

Further, use of quantity data as a measure of output necessarily implies the availability of some quality index weighting factor if such a measure is to have validity, unless perfect homogeneity can be assumed.

For example a barrel of flour milled from non-durum wheat containing wild oats or rye is of a lower quality than, and inhomogeneous with, a barrel of durum wheat flour not containing these contaminants. No indices of quality exist and the census descriptions in general do not permit such inferences. Price as an index of quality is a relatively poor measure since it embodies many other factors such as monopoly rents or shifts in demand or supply.

Finally, many firms are multi-product enterprises and in general there exists no value-free method of allocating inputs of labor, capital and raw materials between these outputs, while quite clearly it is also not possible to sum these quantities together.

As a consequence, value-added is used as the principal measure of output, where value-added is defined to be:

$$VA = PV - RV$$

Where PV is the value of all outputs produced by the firm, and RV is the value of raw materials used. Since there necessarily exists some proportionality between raw materials and output such a transformation removes some potential multicolinearity from the estimation procedure. The value-added measure therefore represents the contribution of labor (including management) and capital.

Unfortunately the use of value-added data (or more generally, the use of dollar data on inputs and outputs) does cloud the distinction between economies of scale and economies of size. Economies of scale are a purely production phenomenon resulting from factors internal to the production process and defined in terms of the degree of homogeneity of the production function. Economies of size on the other hand are external to the production process. Consider, for example, the simple case of a firm subject to constant returns to scale (i.e., a production function homogeneous of degree one) using two factors inputs, labor and capital services. According to the production function a proportionate increase in both labor and capital services will lead to a proportionate increase in output. However, in order to increase the flow of services by that proportionate amount the firm may have to increase its employment of factors by <u>more</u> than that proportionate amount. Clearly if this were the case then average costs would rise despite the presence of constant returns to scale. Economies of size are consequently defined in terms of the shape of the average cost curve. Maintaining the distinction between economies of scale and economies of size permits resolution of the apparent contradiction whereby firms subject to constant returns to scale have indeterminate plant size.[16] Plant size under this distinction is determined by the technological forces internal to the firm and reflected in the economies of scale parameter while optimal firm size is determined by economies of size. Moreover, economies of size will be influenced by such factors as the ability to purchase inputs more cheaply than the competition as a result of local factor market conditions or the exercise of monopsony power or the granting of preferential tariffs for bulk purchases by suppliers.

For a limited subset of single product firms producing essentially homogeneous products—lumber milling, brick making and flour milling—it has proved possible to use quantity rather than value-added data. These results are reported in Chapter 8.

Although many problems plague the use of the manuscript census data most of these differences can be satisfactorily solved. The result, I would argue, is clearly superior to reliance upon the published census data which is quite definitely in error. Consequently one must question the validity of works based upon unquestioning acceptance of the published census such as Albert Niemi's book, State and Regional Patterns in American Manufacturing, 1860-1900. The inaccuracy of our information about the parent population also renders useless our conventional statistical tests and while I do not ask the reader to accept on faith that the Bateman-Weiss samples are superior to any other extant body of data on mid-nineteenth century American manufacturing, the discussion of problems and their resolution in the foregoing, will, I hope, support this claim. Further support in the way of testing the sensitivity of the results to different methods of measurement and estimation is given in Chapter 7 below.

CHAPTER 4

THE ECONOMETRIC INTERPRETATION OF THE PRODUCTION FUNCTION ESTIMATES

Sample sizes, particularly at the regional industry level, were generally adequate for us to have confidence in the results. Twelve was taken to be the minimum acceptable sample size and provided for nine degrees of freedom for the Cobb-Douglas production function estimates and for six degrees of freedom with the unconstrained general polynomial approximation to the CES function. The result was that the vast majority of the regressions "explained" a significant portion of the total variability in the data. Indeed only one of the results reported in this abbreviated summary failed to pass the F-test at the five percent significance level.

However, while almost all regressions "explained" a significant portion of the total variation, none was exceptionally good. Mean square errors, for example, implied a range for the average standard deviation of residuals from as much as 98 percent (poor) to a low of 20 percent (good). Clearly although the regressions "explained" a significant amount of the total variability there remained a great deal of variation that could not be explained by the available variables.

The principal advantage of the CES production function over the simpler Cobb-Douglas is the removal of the constraint of unitary elasticity of substitution. However, the Cobb-Douglas production function generally performed marginally better than the CES in terms of minimizing mean square error even when the evidence pointed to an elasticity of substitution that was significantly different from unity. Where this was true, the implied elasticity of substitution fell within the ranges suggested by Maddala and Kadane[1] as not biasing the estimate of the returns to scale parameter even if the equation is mis-specified. Consequently all results reported here are made using the Cobb-Douglas specification.

Just as there is some evidence of non-unitary elasticity of substitution, some evidence of non-homotheticity was also detected. This was generally weak and in only very few cases were more than one of the key coefficients in Equation IV (Table 2.2) significantly different from zero. In no instance, however, did this specification perform significantly better than the Cobb-Douglas form, while non-homotheticity makes it impossible to specify the returns to scale without simultaneously specifying the technique being used (i.e., the capital-labor ratio) since returns to scale are invariant for a given technique but differ from technique to technique.

As noted in Chapter 2, the marginal products are

$\alpha \cdot \frac{V}{L}$ for labor, and

$\beta \cdot \frac{V}{L}$ for capital in the Cobb-Douglas production function

where α and β are the output elasticities with respect to labor and capital. In general, β, the output elasticity with respect to capital was the most consistently significant variable, being significantly greater than zero at the five percent level in most equations. On the other hand, it was often impossible to reject the hypothesis that the output elasticity with respect to labor was not significantly different from zero.

On the face of it, this result would suggest that the marginal product of capital was significantly positive, while that of labor approached zero. In terms of an isoquant diagram, the typical firm then appears to be operating in the region where the isoquants become parallel to the labor axis. In a two-factor world this would conflict with the labor scarcity hypothesis which predicts that in the U.S. capital was substituted for the relatively more scarce labor so that labor should be used at its extensive rather than its intensive margin. This is discussed in greater detail in Chapters 5, 6 and 7 below.

Because I fit an unconstrained Cobb-Douglas production function, the output elasticities cannot be interpreted as factor shares. However they can be interpreted as indicating relative shares under certain conditions. Under conditions of perfect competition in all markets, labor and capital are paid an equilibrium price equal to the value of their respective marginal productivities and these shares would be exactly equal to the output elasticities. To posit equality between relative shares and the relative output elasticities requires only that we assume that the real factor prices are in uniform proportion to their respective marginal physical products. This would be compatible either with perfect competition or with equal degrees of inperfection in all markets somewhat analogous to Galbraith's theory of countervailing power.[2] That is if S_L and S_K are the respective shares of labor and capital, then

$$S_L/[S_L + S_K] = \alpha/[\alpha + \beta]$$

In cases where the shares of labor and capital can be observed then it is possible to use the data to measure the rate of exploitation of labor where exploitation is defined as the gap between the actual wage rate and the value of the marginal physical product of labor.

Consider Figure 4-1. The firm is a monopsonist in the labor market but a perfect competitor in the product market. Then

$$w = [(\partial Q/\partial L) - e] \cdot P$$

where w is the wage rate, P is the price of output, $\partial Q/\partial L$ is the marginal physical product of labor and e is the amount by which L is paid less than its physical product. The labor share of total costs is then

$$S_L = (w \cdot L/P \cdot Q) = [(\partial Q/\partial L) - e] \cdot (L/Q)$$

But from Chapter 2 we know that

$$\alpha = \frac{\partial Q}{\partial L} \cdot \frac{L}{Q}$$

so that $S_L < \alpha$. Since the product must be exhausted even though this is not guaranteed by our use of an unconstrained Cobb-Douglas function we may use the three foregoing equations to write:

$$\frac{S_L}{1 - S_K} = \alpha/(\alpha + \beta) - [e(L/Q)]/[\alpha + \beta]$$

Figure 4.1

Monopsony in the Labor Market.

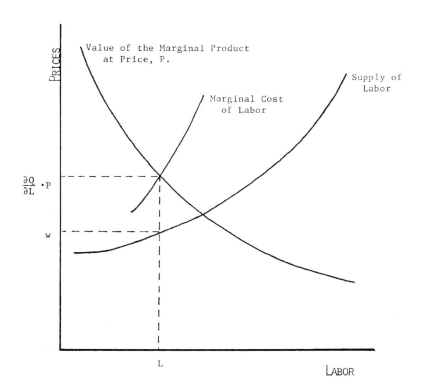

Rearranging

$$\frac{S_L}{1 - S_K} = \frac{\alpha}{(\alpha + \beta)} \cdot [1 - e/(\partial Q/\partial L)]$$

Let $E = e/(Q/L)$, then

$$E = 1 - \left[\frac{(S_L)/(1 - S_K)}{(\alpha)/(\alpha + \beta)} \right]$$

defines the rate of exploitation.[3]

However, our primary interest is in the sum of these output elasticities rather than in the constituent parts. In testing for returns to scale, the null hypothesis is that

$$H_o: \alpha + \beta = 1$$

against the alternative hypothesis:

$$H_a: \alpha + \beta \neq 1$$

Significance level is taken as the five percent level and if the alternative hypothesis is accepted then it is noted whether the scale elasticity is significantly greater than unity or significantly less than unity. It was felt that this testing procedure would be less confusing than some of the other options such as

$$H_o: \alpha + \beta \geq 1$$

and $$H_a: \alpha + \beta < 1$$

or $$H_o: \alpha + \beta \leq 1$$

and $H_a: \alpha + \beta > 1$

which have been used by David,[4] among others.

In the chapters following, the regional production function estimates for the five major manufacturing industries are discussed and analyzed, together with estimates of the aggregate production.

CHAPTER 5

PRODUCTION CONDITIONS FOR INTRA-REGIONALLY TRADED COMMODITIES

In recent years there has been a growing awareness that in the middle of the nineteenth century, the relevant market for most firms, in most industries, was the area in the immediate vicinity of the plant.[1] Most products were locally produced and consumed rather than entering into inter-regional trade.

As recently as 1963, the Census Bureau identified some fifty-four industries that served primarily regional markets such as malt liquor, wooden furniture, meat processing, sawmills and planning mills, printers and gray iron foundaries.[2] Each of these industries was active during the nineteenth century. Classified as predominantly local manufacturing industries were dairy products, baking and brick manufacture.[3] These industries produced about one-quarter of all the U.S. manufacturing value-added in 1963.[4] Adding to this list of local and regional industries flour and grist milling which, notwithstanding the growth of export-oriented centers such as Richmond, Va., Chicago, Il., and Minneapolis, Mn., remained a predominantly local industry widely dispersed across the country would show the results given in Table 5.1 for the period 1850-1870. Just these ten local and regional industries produced over twenty percent of manufacturing value-added over this period and if all industries were classified as local/regional or national then it is likely that the local and regional industries would produce close to

TABLE 5.1

THE RELATIVE IMPORTANCE OF LOCAL AND REGIONAL MANUFACTURING
INDUSTRIES IN THE U.S., 1850–1870

	INDUSTRY	VALUE-ADDED AS A PERCENTAGE OF TOTAL U.S.		
		1850	1860	1870
I.	LOCAL INDUSTRIES			
	Bread and Bakery	1.06%	0.74%	0.85%
	Brick	1.11	0.96	1.24
	Dairy Products	0.00	0.00	0.23
	Flour and Grist	4.96	4.69	4.45
	Lumber	6.67	6.27	6.90
II.	REGIONAL INDUSTRIES			
	Furniture	2.49	2.04	2.48
	Iron Castings	2.50	2.47	2.14
	Malt Liquor	1.11	1.32	1.58
	Meat Processing	0.55	0.83	0.66
	Printing	1.43	2.13	2.40
Σ Local + Regional		21.88	21.45	22.93

Source: Seventh Census (1859)
Eighth Census (1863)
Ninth Census (1872)

one-half of the total value-added. Two industries, flour milling and lumber milling account for about 11 percent of total U.S. manufacturing value-added and these two industries will be the principal focus here.

The definition of the extent of the market is important for determining the extent of actual or potential monopoly power which is expressed in terms of control over the relevant market. For example both lumber and flour mills were the most geographically dispersed of all industries and were also the most widely owned. At least one firm out of five was either a lumber mill or a flour mill.[5] It might therefore be argued that given the large number of plants producing a relatively homogeneous commodity, either of these industries should approximate the economist's definition of a perfectly competitive industry. In fact the largest plant in each industry produced an average of 8 percent of the industry output in each state and it is probable that treating the state as the market, overstates the true extent of the market for firms in these industries.[6] According to Bateman and Weiss

> Given the antebellum South's poor overland transport facilities, its dispersed and predominantly rural population, the nature of most of its manufactured products (heavy, low-valued relative to weight, natural resource intensive), its sales distribution methods, and the imperfect market information channels, one could anticipate that for most products even a state market definition would overstate actual market size as viewed by most buyers and sellers.[7]

If this was true of the South it was almost certainly true of the mid-West and the Pacific West until after the Civil War with the completion of most railroad links.

Even in later years, despite the growth of larger scale plants in those industries which catered to a national market, most lumber or flour mills remained local monopolies or near-monopolies. This reflected the importance of transportation costs in the price of a product with a relatively low value-to-weight ratio and where locational advantages were minimal.

To the extent that these products were only traded intra-regionally, the Genovese hypothesis as discussed in Chapter 1 is irrelevant so far as flour and lumber milling are concerned.[8] On the other hand because these two industries are so typical of mid-nineteenth century manufacturing, the results might be regarded as more important than those for inter-regionally traded commodities such as are discussed in the next chapter.

I. Flour Milling

As indicated above, the available evidence suggests that flour milling was not perfectly competitive even before the growth of the national milling firms and the development of Minneapolis as a flour milling center. Bateman and Weiss[9] estimate that in 1850 the largest flour mill in an eastern or southern state produced 8-9 percent of the state's output--compared with an average of only 3 percent in the mid-western states. Concentration increased in later years with the average single firm concentration ratio for eastern and southern states rising to 11-12 percent by 1860 and to 4 percent in the mid-West.

During the course of the nineteenth century the geographic center of the nation's wheat production shifted westward with the westward movement. In the 1850s it was in Ohio, by the 1860s in Indiana and by the 1870s it had reached Springfield, Illinois.[10] This westward movement

together with a spreading railroad network shifted flour production in
favor of the western states although eastern and southern mills remained
in business to satisfy local demand. Despite this, some large mills remained in business on the east coast in New York and Virginia such as
Haxall Mills or Warwick and Barksdale of Richmond where they supplied
foreign markets and benefited from their proximity to port facilities.
These Richmond, Virginia mills were the largest in the country until the
construction of the Washburn Mills at Minneapolis and were capable of
grinding between 700 and 900 barrels of flour a day.[11] There is evidence
though that these large mills suffered from diseconomies of size as
Kuhlmann reports complaints that 'there is not a regular supply of wheat
to keep them at work throughout the year.'[12]

Technological change in flour milling over the period seems to have
been minimal. Most large mills mimicked the Haxall design and virtually
all made some use of Oliver Evans' improved machinery.[13] The waterwheel
was gradually replaced by the water turbine or the steam engine which
reduced the amount of gearing necessary for efficient milling, but the
basic process still relied upon the millstone with its frequent need
for redressing and need for constant attention. The so-called "New
Process" in which the millstones were replaced by rollers which did 30
percent more work and used 47 percent less power than stones did not
come into use until the early 1870s.[14] Technological change can therefore be discounted over this period.

Flour milling was, throughout the period, a seasonal industry.
Even large mills such as those of the Richmond area had difficulty in
securing adequate supplies to operate year round. The seasonality was

reinforced where the power source was water for added to the periodic scarcity of wheat, corn and other grains were the seasonal fluctuations in river stages with summer drought and winter freeze. Indeed, according to the Census Bureau, as late as 1890, flour mills only operated an average of seven months a year[15] and a job in a flour mill was frequently combined with some other occupation.

The extent to which flour (and lumber) milling was a local industry drawing upon part-time and seasonal labor may help explain the production function estimates for the flour milling industry. Estimates for 1850 are given in Table 5.2, those for 1860, in Table 5.3 and those for 1870, in Table 5.4.

Given the limited extent of the market one would expect that the typical flour mill would be a small scale operation operating under conditions of constant or increasing returns to scale depending upon how well the plant was adapted to market conditions. With the exception of the estimate for the Pacific region flour mills in 1850, these expectations are fulfilled. For the United States as a whole, there is evidence that in each census year the industry was operating under conditions of increasing returns to scale and decreasing unit costs. A ten percent increase in both labor and capital would increase output by between 11.6 and 12.8 percent. In the sub-regions, the southern flour milling industry in 1860 was the only other where scale economies were sufficiently pronounced to be significant.

The west coast flour mills according to our estimates for 1850 were operating on too large a scale in the region of decreasing returns. They

TABLE 5.2

ORDINARY LEAST SQUARES ESTIMATES OF THE PRODUCTION FUNCTION FOR
FLOUR MILLING
CENSUS YEAR 1850
(T-STATISTIC)

REGION	INTERCEPT TERM	COEFFICIENT OF LABOR (1)	COEFFICIENT OF CAPITAL (2)	ECONOMIES OF SCALE (2)	F-RATIO
MIDDLE ATLANTIC	-.15	.19 (1.90)	.83* (9.02)	1.02 (.32)	126.72
NEW ENGLAND	.65	.52 (1.41)	.70* (4.41)	1.22 (.59)	12.55
PACIFIC	4.93	-.42 (-1.21)	.51 (1.73)	.09** (-2.50)	1.68
SOUTHERN	2.66	.65* (3.67)	.46* (5.39)	1.11 (.72)	42.81
WESTERN	2.19	.48* (2.26)	.59* (4.12)	1.08 (.53)	40.00
THE UNITED STATES	1.13	.53* (5.36)	.68* (13.20)	1.21* (2.68)	231.77

FOOTNOTES—

(1) The coefficient is compared with a value of zero for tests of significance
(2) The coefficient is compared with a value of one for tests of significance
* Coefficient significantly greater than zero (or one) at the five percent level
** Coefficient significantly less than zero (or one) at the five percent level

In regions not appearing, sample size was too small
Regions as described in Chapter 3.

SOURCE—

Derived from the Bateman-Weiss samples.

TABLE 5.3

ORDINARY LEAST SQUARES ESTIMATES OF THE PRODUCTION FUNCTION FOR
FLOUR MILLING
CENSUS YEAR 1860
(T-STATISTIC)

REGION	INTERCEPT TERM	COEFFICIENT LABOR (1)	COEFFICIENT CAPITAL (1)	ECONOMIES OF SCALE (2)	F-RATIO
MIDDLE ATLANTIC	.07	.27 (1.12)	.82* (5.55)	1.09 (.52)	42.28
NEW ENGLAND	-3.28	-.11 (-.27)	1.22* (5.81)	1.10 (.36)	43.10
PACIFIC	-1.83	.21 (.70)	1.06* (4.80)	1.28 (4.72)	18.42
SOUTHERN	1.55	.73* (7.17)	.64* (11.17)	1.37* (4.72)	239.69
WESTERN	2.62	.66* (4.43)	.52* (5.56)	1.18 (1.70)	82.54
THE UNITED STATES	1.26	.60* (8.18)	.68* (16.68)	1.28* (5.17)	504.10

FOOTNOTES--
 SEE TABLE 5.2

SOURCE--
 DERIVED FROM THE BATEMAN-WEISS SAMPLES

TABLE 5.4

ORDINARY LEAST SQUARES ESTIMATES OF THE PRODUCTION FUNCTION FOR
FLOUR MILLING
CENSUS YEAR 1870
(T-STATISTIC)

REGION	INTERCEPT TERM	COEFFICIENT OF LABOR (1)	COEFFICIENT OF CAPITAL (1)	ECONOMIES OF SCALE (2)	F-RATIO
MIDDLE ATLANTIC	-1.04	.28 (1.29)	.92* (3.77)	1.21 (1.50)	38.53
NEW ENGLAND	-.56	.23 (1.84)	.86* (7.30)	1.09 (1.29)	141.21
PACIFIC	-1.13	-.20 (-.56)	1.00* (7.44)	.80 (-.70)	42.00
SOUTHERN	.40	.29* (3.56)	.80* (15.74)	1.09 (1.19)	196.69
WESTERN	1.11	.62* (2.74)	.69* (4.98)	1.32 (1.75)	38.25
THE UNITED STATES	.45	.38* (4.87)	.78* (22.38)	1.16* (2.34)	393.42

FOOTNOTES--
  SEE TABLE 5.2

SOURCE--
  DERIVED FROM THE BATEMAN-WEISS SAMPLES

were also, on the average, larger than the typical flour mill in other regions. If there existed some optimum size, given the level of technology and the extent of the market as limited by the transport system, then it would seem that the Pacific coast flour mills were too large in 1850 but that these constraints had eased by 1860. From the econometric standpoint, however, this regression equation for the Pacific coast flour mills is the least satisfactory of all estimates and hence we may be erecting strawmen.

There is, however, a unity about the estimates for flour milling that is to be found in the individual output elasticities. The output elasticity with respect to capital is generally significantly positive indicating that the marginal product of capital was probably quite high and certainly was significantly positive. On the other hand, in New England, the Middle Atlantic states and in the Pacific region, the output elasticity with respect to labor was not significantly different from zero. In these regions labor appears to have been used at its intensive margin and capital, not labor, is imposing a binding constraint upon the amount of output that can be produced. This would be consistent with a number of hypotheses. One would be that ex post the smooth and continuous and differentiable production function comes to approximate a Leontief fixed coefficient production function. In such a case, attempting to increase production in the short-run by using more labor with the fixed amount of capital would result in no increase in output. Alternatively one might view the apparently low productivity of labor as reflecting a shortage of other part-time occupations in the regions with which the flour milling job may be combined. As a result, labor was underemployed year round in a seasonal business. In the South and mid-West on the other hand farming and flour milling (or some other such combination) reduced the level of labor surplus. Something of a similar phenomenon is to be found in lumber milling.

II. Lumber Milling

Like the flour milling industry, lumber milling at least until the 1870s was a geographically dispersed local industry with few major firms. Large lumber concerns such as Weyerhaeuser or the Daniel Shaw Lumber Company were still in their infancy and did not begin to exert much influence in the industry until later. At the same time there is evidence that the local sawmill had a protected position in its local area and Bateman and Weiss give the average state single firm concentration ratios in this industry of the order of 6-19 percent.[16]

The period 1850-1870 marks the shift of the lumber industry from northern New England (especially Maine) into the hardwood and white pine area of the Great Lakes, into the yellow pinelands of the South and the beginnings of a Pacific coast industry based on the Redwood and the Douglas Fir. This shift further removed the industry from the major population centers increasing dependency upon local markets and transportation.

Evidence of technological change is slight. Most lumbermills located along rivers and streams down which the logs were floated. Consequently there was a natural inclination to rely upon waterpower. The seasonal nature of this power source did not inhibit the lumber industry for the period when the river was frozen or the water level to low was

also the period when no new lumber was arriving at the mill. Use of
waterwheel however did inhibit the adoption of the circular saw which
relied on high operating speeds found only with the turbine or the steam
engine. The circular saw replacing the muley or sash saw more than
doubled labor productivity over earlier vertical saw designs by pre-
senting a continuous cutting edge to the log and being thinner hence
producing less sawdust or kerf.[17] More fundamental change had to await
the development of the band-saw in the 1860's (which removed the constraint on log size) and the gang-saw (which made multiple board cuts
in a single pass). It is doubtful whether more than a small fraction
of plants were using these inventions before the 1870s.

The estimates for the lumber milling production functions in 1850,
1860 and 1870 are given in Tables 5.5, 5.6 and 5.7 respectively. The
evidence on scale economies points to constant or increasing returns
depending upon the region and year. Most consistent among the scale
findings are increasing returns to scale for the south and for the
nation as a whole. In these cases both output elasticities were significantly positive. In the south this may reflect the more favorable
climatic conditions. Aside from the persistence of increasing returns
to scale in southern lumber mills and for the nation, variations in
scale economies seem to be non-systematic.

The output elasticity with respect to capital was uniformly significantly positive suggesting that the marginal product of capital was
high and that the amount of capital invested imposed one of the binding
constraints upon the level of output. This is certainly true for those

TABLE 5.5
ORDINARY LEAST SQUARES ESTIMATES OF THE PRODUCTION FUNCTION FOR
LUMBER MILLING
CENSUS YEAR 1850
(T-STATISTIC)

REGION	INTERCEPT TERM	COEFFICIENT OF LABOR (1)	COEFFICIENT OF CAPITAL (1)	ECONOMIES OF SCALE (2)	F-RATIO
MIDDLE ATLANTIC	1.30	.24 (1.80)	.69* (6.42)	.93 (-.90)	87.01
NEW ENGLAND	1.42	.32* (4.30)	.66* (9.42)	.98 (-.45)	257.39
PACIFIC	-1.76	-.01 (-.04)	1.15* (8.96)	1.14 (1.00)	59.32
SOUTHERN	1.04	.46* (5.68)	.71* (10.84)	1.17* (3.52)	300.67
WESTERN	-.56	.09 (.90)	.96* (10.00)	1.05 (.78)	149.53
THE UNITED STATES	-.39	.22* (5.21)	.92* (28.18)	1.14* (5.01)	1137.08

FOOTNOTES--
SEE TABLE 5.2

SOURCE--
DERIVED FROM THE BATEMAN-WEISS SAMPLES

TABLE 5.6

ORDINARY LEAST SQUARES ESTIMATES OF THE PRODUCTION FUNCTION FOR
LUMBER MILLING
CENSUS YEAR 1860
(T-STATISTIC)

REGION	INTERCEPT TERM	COEFFICIENT OF LABOR (1)	COEFFICIENT OF CAPITAL (1)	ECONOMIES OF SCALE (2)	F-RATIO
MIDDLE ATLANTIC	.67	.47* (3.68)	.73* (6.77)	1.28* (2.66)	139.36
NEW ENGLAND	-.69	.14 (1.25)	.93* (9.45)	1.07 (1.21)	197.91
PACIFIC	-3.71	-.10 (-1.23)	1.36* (18.56)	1.26* (3.85)	262.47
SOUTHERN	2.48	.61* (10.76)	.53* (10.65)	1.14* (4.21)	605.20
WESTERN	.18	.32* (4.51)	.83* (13.92)	1.15* (3.63)	450.86
THE UNITED STATES	.55	.40*	.78*	1.18*	1563.58

FOOTNOTES--
   SEE TABLE 5.2

SOURCE--
   DERIVED FROM THE BATEMAN-WEISS SAMPLES

TABLE 5.7
ORDINARY LEAST SQUARES ESTIMATES OF THE PRODUCTION FUNCTION FOR
LUMBER MILLING
CENSUS YEAR 1870
(T-STATISTIC)

REGION	INTERCEPT TERM	COEFFICIENT OF LABOR (1)	COEFFICIENT OF CAPITAL (1)	ECONOMIES OF SCALE (2)	F-RATIO
MIDDLE ATLANTIC	-1.66	.05 (.24)	1.06* (6.58)	1.11 (.68)	36.47
NEW ENGLAND	-.06	.26* (3.02)	.85* (11.88)	1.11* (2.23)	325.51
PACIFIC	.76	.31* (2.38)	.76* (7.74)	1.07 (1.02)	176.75
SOUTHERN	.64	.49* (6.68)	.76* (12.49)	1.26* (4.85)	318.00
WESTERN	.64	.22* (2.52)	.80* (10.49)	1.02 (.25)	163.37
THE UNITED STATES	.81	.42* (10.30)	.74* (22.13)	1.16* (5.60)	914.22

FOOTNOTES--
  SEE TABLE 5.2

SOURCE--
  DERIVED FROM THE BATEMAN-WEISS SAMPLES

regions where the output elasticity with respect to labor was approximately zero.

As noted above in the discussion of flour milling, the later condition may reflect an *ex post* production function that approximates a Leontief fixed coefficients production function or it may reflect the seasonal, part-time nature of the industry in which labor is substituted for capital. The frequency with which the labor coefficient is approximately zero declines over time. This would be consistent with the growth of larger, more capitalistic ventures oriented away from the immediate local market and with the reduction in seasonality contingent upon the spread of the steam engine.

Overall for these two local industries the evidence points to a fairly general failure to attain sufficient scale in many areas to operate under conditions of constant returns. The presence of increasing returns to scale is not, however, a feature solely of southern industry. In both the flour milling and lumber milling industries there is a tendency for the marginal productivity of labor to approach zero and for capital to seem to pose a binding constraint. This may reflect the limited possibilities for substituting labor for capital within these processes or it could reflect the seasonal and part-time nature of the work which the low marginal productivity somewhat irrelevant coupled with an acute shortage of capital due to reliance upon local sources. As we shall see below the converse of these explanations seem to hold in the production of inter-regionally traded goods.

CHAPTER 6

PRODUCTION CONDITIONS FOR INTER-REGIONALLY TRADED COMMODITIES

One of the more frequently discussed aspects of nineteenth century development is the emergence of a national market. However it is doubtful whether such a market existed in the middle of the century for more than a very limited range of products, among which should be listed boots and shoes, ready-made clothing, cotten textiles and machinery. This chapter will focus on the first three of these because of the limited number of observations of machinery manufacturers.

Evidence of a national market especially for boots and shoes and for cotten textiles is quite pronounced. From an early date, the boot and shoe industry specialized both geographically and between firms. In Massachusetts for example, the city of Lynn specialized in women's shoes, Danvers in children's shoes and Marlboro in the production of men's footwear.[1] These New England shoes were produced for the mass market and sold for a dollar a pair.[2] In order to seek orders, the larger factories established branches or marketing centers in other regions. For example as early as 1837 the Batchelor Brothers of Brookfield, Mass. opened a branch in Mobile, Ala. to facilitate sales to the plantations[3] but as other markets developed in the west similar operations were started there.[4] Neither southern or western boot and shoe manufacturers appear to have challenged the status of the New England factories in the mass market. Rather the southern and western

105

producers produced more expensive footwear retailing for about $3.50 a pair in the 1850s and 1860s.[5] It is not clear that these two kinds of footwear are perfect substitutes for each other. The New England product was machine-made, mass-produced and standardized, while that produced elsewhere was custom-made by hand. It is also not clear which was the superior product, at least in terms of durability.[6]

Genovese's argument of southern non-competitiveness focused upon the cotton textile industry and the penetration of the southern market by the New England mills some of which specialized in the production of "negro cloth."[7] It is here that we must look to resolve the three issues raised in Chapter 1. However, there is also evidence that southern cotton mills especially those in South Carolina and Georgia specialized in the production of coarse cottons for the domestic market.[8] Further it is also claimed that these cottons sold readily in the northern urban areas of Baltimore, Philadelphia and New York.[9] Governor Hammond of South Carolina for example claimed, in his address to the South Carolina Institute, that:

> "Already the South, through the almost unnoticed enterprise of a few of her citizens, more than supplies her own consumption of course (sic) cottons, and ships both yarns and cloths with fair profit, to northern markets . . . we have driven [the northern states] from our markets and have already commenced the contest with them for their own in the only class of goods we have yet attempted."[10]

Analysis of these three industries is, however, complicated by technological change, for whereas technological change was minimal in the local industries, notably flour and lumber milling, it appears to have been important in the manufacture of boots and shoes, ready-made clothing and cottons. This technological change makes it difficult, if not impossible, to compare the production function estimates from decade to decade. Including time as a variable in the production function and estimating using observation across the three census years resulted in estimates of a significant coefficient for the time variable which has been interpreted as evidence of technological change.

Technological change in the boot and shoe industry stemmed from the breakdown of complex hand operations into simpler but more numerous machine operations so that "between 1850 and 1900 the shoe industry was transformed from one in which the only aids were a lap-stone, a hammer, and an awl, to one in which 300 machines were necessary to make all the different styles of footwear in use, and at least 28 machines and sometimes twice the number were required to produce one shoe."[11] This mechanization proceeded most rapidly in New England and more slowly elsewhere. The principal agency behind the mechanization of the boot and shoe industry was the sewing machine:[12]

> That (the sewing machine) and other labor-saving machines for cutting out the soles, heels and uppers, for pegging, burnishing, and other operations, are now driven by the exhaustless energy of steam, whereby the entire system of manufactures has been imperceptibly but effectually revolutionized. Their use has silently brought about a transfer of work from small shops to large factories, several stories high, in which all parts of the manufacture are carried on under the same roof, each floor being devoted to a separate portion of the work.

The impact of the sewing machine was also felt in the clothing industry where numerous improvements to the sewing machine such as the hemming guide developed by S. P. Chapin of New York in 1856 and guides for button-holing developed by Otis Avery the same year increased specialization and the rate of diffusion.[13] Despite the great labor-savings permitted by the sewing machine, "each of which is estimated by the proprietors for shirt front and collar manufactories employing from thirty to seventy-five machines each, to save the labor of ten persons,"[14] the high initial cost of about $125 for the most basic treadle operated Howe machine discourged their use in the small factories and shops.[15]

The origin, nature and extent of technological change in the cotton textile industry is harder to pin-point, though much was doubtless due to the continued improvement of the power loom and of spinning machinery which accounted for much of the earlier growth.[16]

I. Boots and Shoes

The most notable features of the boot and shoe industry estimates given in Tables 6.1-6.3 are, first, the appearance of significant decreasing returns to scale in this industry in each year for the nation as a whole in contrast with approximately constant (albeit marginally decreasing) returns at the regional level. The results show little change from year to year.

Second, output elasticities with respect to both labor and capital are generally significantly positive. Given the interpretation we have made in Chapter 5 above, this would seem to imply considerable opportunities to substitute labor for capital and vice versa rather than a fixed coefficient-type production function. Neither factor appears to have been used at or near its extensive margin.

Third, with the exception of the New England estimates, the output elasticities with respect to labor are essentially similar. These would imply a labor share in value added of about 50-60 percent in 1850 rising

TABLE 6.1

ORDINARY LEAST SQUARES ESTIMATES OF THE PRODUCTION FUNCTION FOR
BOOTS AND SHOES
CENSUS YEAR 1850
(T-STATISTIC)

REGION	INTERCEPT TERM	COEFFICIENT OF LABOR (1)	CAPITAL (1)	ECONOMIES OF SCALE (2)	F-RATIO
MIDDLE ATLANTIC	3.92	.59* (7.89)	.35* (5.22)	.94 (-1.44)	258.94
NEW ENGLAND	1.39	.23* (3.12)	.75* (9.61)	.98 (-.67)	525.78
SOUTHERN	3.62	.52* (4.38)	.41* (4.57)	.93 (-1.00)	88.94
WESTERN	4.62	.80* (5.66)	.23 (1.75)	1.03 (.39)	106.45
THE UNITED STATES	3.45	.51* (11.28)	.43* (10.23)	.93** (-2.91)	879.49

FOOTNOTES--
    SEE TABLE 5.2

SOURCE--
    DERIVED FROM THE BATEMAN-WEISS SAMPLES

109

TABLE 6.2
ORDINARY LEAST SQUARES ESTIMATES OF THE PRODUCTION FUNCTION FOR
BOOTS AND SHOES
CENSUS YEAR 1860
(T-STATISTIC)

REGION	INTERCEPT TERM	COEFFICIENT OF LABOR (1)	COEFFICIENT OF CAPITAL (1)	ECONOMIES OF SCALE (2)	F-RATIO
MIDDLE ATLANTIC	4.23	.70* (8.73)	.31* (4.36)	1.01 (.27)	312.24
NEW ENGLAND	2.10	.30* (2.75)	.64* (6.26)	.95 (-1.23)	270.90
PACIFIC	5.18	.70* (2.53)	.27 (1.70)	.98 (-.09)	10.05
SOUTHERN	4.32	.69* (7.35)	.29* (3.92)	.99 (-.22)	110.31
WESTERN	4.34	.81* (7.99)	.28* (3.55)	1.09 (1.49)	163.33
THE UNITED STATES	3.81	.56* (12.14)	.39* (9.55)	.95** (-2.25)	916.88

FOOTNOTES--
SEE TABLE 5.2

SOURCE--
DERIVED FROM THE BATEMAN-WEISS SAMPLES

TABLE 6.3

ORDINARY LEAST SQUARES ESTIMATES OF THE PRODUCTION FUNCTION FOR
BOOTS AND SHOES
CENSUS YEAR 1870
(T-STATISTIC)

REGION	INTERCEPT TERM	COEFFICIENT OF LABOR (1)	COEFFICIENT OF CAPITAL (1)	ECONOMIES OF SCALE (2)	F-RATIO
MIDDLE ATLANTIC	3.50	.42* (3.57)	.51* (5.75)	.93 (-.96)	122.58
NEW ENGLAND	.89	.14 (1.32)	.85* (9.36)	.98 (-.35)	309.47
PACIFIC	2.39	.41* (3.73)	.67* (8.08)	1.08 (.85)	88.42
SOUTHERN	3.05	.53* (3.54)	.54* (6.16)	1.07 (.70)	125.79
WESTERN	2.56	.26 (1.84)	.61* (6.29)	.87 (-1.60)	90.25
THE UNITED STATES	2.79	.35* (6.37)	.59* (14.55)	.94** (-2.01)	719.27

FOOTNOTES--
 SEE TABLE 5.2

SOURCE--
 DERIVED FROM THE BATEMAN-WEISS SAMPLES

to 70-80 percent in 1860 before slipping back to 45-50 percent by 1870. The labor share in New England is much smaller and may reflect that mechanization was most advanced in this region. It may well be that technological change radically altered the shape of the isoquants and that mechanization reduced the size of production opportunities. Certainly the output elasticity with respect to capital was significantly greater in New England than in the other regions.

II. Clothing

Estimates for the clothing industry are given in Tables 6.4-6.6 and once again they show constant or decreasing returns to scale across the regions for this industry, with significant decreasing returns in the nation in 1860 and 1870 and in the mid-West in 1860. The output elasticity with respect to capital was uniformly significantly positive unlike that for labor. Interpretation of the labor coefficient is difficult because of the wide variation in the estimate between regions. This may in fact reflect a similarly wide diversity in production methods both within and between regions. Results for the South are especially confused and little weight is given to them. More research is necessary on this industry before we can reach a definite conclusion. Based on the distribution of sewing machine manufactories, however, the new technology and organization based on this invention emerged first in the Middle Atlantic and New England states and migrated westward rather than southwards. Such a pattern is not apparent in the estimates.

TABLE 6.4

ORDINARY LEAST SQUARES ESTIMATES OF THE PRODUCTION FUNCTION FOR CLOTHING
CENSUS YEAR 1850
(T-STATISTIC)

REGION	INTERCEPT TERM	COEFFICIENT OF LABOR (1)	COEFFICIENT OF CAPITAL (1)	ECONOMIES OF SCALE (2)	F-RATIO
MIDDLE ATLANTIC	1.00	.30* (2.44)	.75* (6.51)	1.06 (.94)	167.45
NEW ENGLAND	0.00	.22 (.75)	.87* (3.05)	1.09 (.46)	16.95
SOUTHERN	4.64	.66* (4.12)	.24* (2.23)	.89 (-1.13)	56.44
WESTERN	1.68	.18 (.90)	.71* (3.17)	.89 (-1.08)	38.13
THE UNITED STATES	2.42	.39* (4.33)	.56* (6.92)	.95 (-1.03)	197.20

FOOTNOTES--
    SEE TABLE 5.2
SOURCE--
    DERIVED FROM THE BATEMAN-WEISS SAMPLES

TABLE 6.5
ORDINARY LEAST SQUARES ESTIMATES OF THE PRODUCTION FUNCTION FOR
CLOTHING
CENSUS YEAR 1860
(T-STATISTIC)

REGION	INTERCEPT TERM	COEFFICIENT OF LABOR (1)	COEFFICIENT OF CAPITAL (1)	ECONOMIES OF SCALE (2)	F-RATIO
MIDDLE ATLANTIC	.66	.07 (.56)	.85* (7.65)	.91 (-1.44)	134.26
NEW ENGLAND	.28	.13 (1.38)	.90* (7.87)	1.02 (.34)	116.47
SOUTHERN	-1.84	-.53** (-2.43)	1.30* (7.16)	.77 (-1.87)	43.68
WESTERN	2.38	.20 (1.41)	.63* (4.23)	.83** (-2.38)	65.15
THE UNITED STATES	.50	.03 (.48)	.89* (13.84)	.92** (-2.32)	350.70

FOOTNOTES—
    SEE TABLE 5.2
SOURCE—
    DERIVED FROM THE BATEMAN-WEISS SAMPLES

TABLE 6.6
ORDINARY LEAST SQUARES ESTIMATES OF THE PRODUCTION FUNCTION FOR
CLOTHING
CENSUS YEAR 1870
(T-STATISTIC)

REGION	INTERCEPT TERM	COEFFICIENT OF LABOR (1)	COEFFICIENT OF CAPITAL (1)	ECONOMIES OF SCALE (2)	F-RATIO
MIDDLE ATLANTIC	1.76	.30 (1.33)	.69* (4.59)	1.00 (-.03)	83.88
NEW ENGLAND	2.57	.42* (3.23)	.56* (5.06)	.97 (-.45)	141.01
PACIFIC	.87	.13 (1.55)	.84* (9.87)	.98 (-.24)	73.03
SOUTHERN	2.69	.45* (2.25)	.57* (4.45)	1.01 (.08)	35.02
WESTERN	1.52	.16 (1.15)	.72* (5.52)	.88 (-1.76)	92.38
THE UNITED STATES	1.75	.23* (3.90)	.70* (14.11)	.93** (-2.04)	444.18

FOOTNOTES--
    SEE TABLE 5.2

SOURCE--
    DERIVED FROM THE BATEMAN-WEISS SAMPLES

II. Cotton Textiles

The estimates for cotton textiles are given in Tables 6.7-6.9. As the number of separate estimates indicates, sample sizes for cotton mills were rather small especially as one travelled further west where the emphasis was upon the production of woolens rather than cottons.[17] Indeed in 1870 no region met our minimum sample size criterion.

The results uniformly indicate constant or decreasing returns to scale across all regions and years, although the decreasing returns were only significant in the national estimate for 1850 where a ten percent increase in both labor and capital would have raised output by only 8.1 percent. This conclusion is the same as that arrived at by Zevin[18] and David[19] using the Baker Library sample of Massachusetts cotton mills used by McGouldrick.[20]

Despite differences between our estimates of the output elasticities the 1860 estimate of labor's share (as shown in Chapter 4) is 0.438, quite close to that estimated by Zevin and David.[21] These estimates of the cotton textile production function are therefore supported by independent observations.

It is impossible on the basis of these estimates to reject the hypothesis that southern mills faced the same production function as the New England mills. To the extent that many southern cotton mills employed as consulting engineers men pirated from the more famous New England mills, any similarities should not be surprising.[22]

The evidence presented above sheds light upon what I have called (in Chapter 1) the third Russel-Linden-Genovese hypothesis that southern

TABLE 6.7
ORDINARY LEAST SQUARES ESTIMATES OF THE PRODUCTION FUNCTION FOR
COTTON GOODS
CENSUS YEAR 1850
(T-STATISTIC)

REGION	INTERCEPT TERM	COEFFICIENT OF LABOR (1)	COEFFICIENT OF CAPITAL (1)	ECONOMIES OF SCALE (2)	F-RATIO
NEW ENGLAND	.64	-.09 (-.23)	.84* (2.18)	.75 (-1.85)	15.81
SOUTHERN	2.26	.18 (.65)	.57* (3.03)	.75 (-2.03)	53.05
THE UNITED STATES	1.95	.20 (1.15)	.61* (3.85)	.81** (-2.76)	75.86

FOOTNOTES--
  SEE TABLE 5.2

SOURCE--
  DERIVED FROM THE BATEMAN-WEISS SAMPLES

TABLE 6.8

ORDINARY LEAST SQUARES ESTIMATES OF THE PRODUCTION FUNCTION FOR
COTTON GOODS
CENSUS YEAR 1860
(T-STATISTIC)

REGION	INTERCEPT TERM	COEFFICIENT OF LABOR (1)	COEFFICIENT OF CAPITAL (1)	ECONOMIES OF SCALE (2)	F-RATIO
MIDDLE ATLANTIC	3.89	.53 (1.28)	.35 (1.12)	.88 (-.80)	32.04
NEW ENGLAND	2.45	.42* (2.62)	.54* (2.99)	.96 (-.67)	119.20
SOUTHERN	4.46	.36 (.78)	.35 (.89)	.72 (-1.20)	5.08
THE UNITED STATES	3.34	.48* (3.67)	.42* (3.23)	.90 (-1.83)	146.61

FOOTNOTES--
SEE TABLE 5.2

SOURCE--
DERIVED FROM THE BATEMAN-WEISS SAMPLES

TABLE 6.9
ORDINARY LEAST SQUARES ESTIMATES OF THE PRODUCTION FUNCTION FOR
COTTON GOODS
CENSUS YEAR 1870
(T-STATISTIC)

REGION	INTERCEPT TERM	COEFFICIENT OF LABOR (1)	COEFFICIENT OF CAPITAL (1)	ECONOMIES OF SCALE (2)	F-RATIO
THE UNITED STATES	3.66	.67* (2.61)	.34 (1.56)	1.01 (.13)	39.07

FOOTNOTES--
  SEE TABLE 5.2

SOURCE--
  DERIVED FROM THE BATEMAN-WEISS SAMPLES

firms operated under increasing returns to scale while northern enterprises produced under conditions of constant returns to scale and constant unit cost having exploited all scale economies and we used null hypothesis (c) (from Chapter 1) to test this. The Russel-Linden-Genovese thesis failed this test. As shown above, in the production of inter-regionally traded commodities there is <u>no evidence</u> of increasing returns to scale. Scale was either constant or decreasing and there was little to choose between the returns to scale estimates for the south or north or, in fact, between any of the regions. The remaining two hypotheses of the Russel-Linden-Genovese await discussion in Chapter 9 below.

CHAPTER 7

THE AGGREGATE REGIONAL PRODUCTION FUNCTION

Estimates of the aggregate production function are dependent upon the industrial mix and structure in each region and it is not clear whether these estimates can be compared between regions or between years. Nor is it clear, at least in an econometric sense, how such results are to be interpreted. However the aggregate production function does provide a convenient means by which the typical production conditions can be characterized within a region despite the restrictions upon it.

I. Census Year 1850

The Middle Atlantic, Pacific and Southern regions all had significant diseconomies of scale in 1850 on the basis of the estimates in Table 7.1. Indeed at a ten percent level of significance, the hypothesis of constant returns to scale would not be rejected in favor of the alternate hypothesis of decreasing returns only for the mid-West.

To the extent that each region was dominated by just two industries, flour and lumber milling where we found only one instance of decreasing returns (in Chapter 5) for the Pacific region, the general finding of diseconomies of scale does not appear to stem from the regression fallacy. It is unlikely that the existence of decreasing returns to scale in a particular industry even an important one, concentrated in a given region can "explain" this finding.

TABLE 7.1

ORDINARY LEAST SQUARES ESTIMATES OF THE AGGREGATE PRODUCTION FUNCTION FOR EACH REGION
CENSUS YEAR 1850
(T-RATIO)

REGION	INTERCEPT TERM	COEFFICIENT OF LABOR (1)	COEFFICIENT OF CAPITAL (1)	ECONOMIES OF SCALE (2)	F-RATIO	SAMPLE SIZE
MIDDLE ATLANTIC	3.06	.49* (20.11)	.47* (24.64)	.96** (-2.11)	1668.95	1187.
NEW ENGLAND	2.75	.47* (18.00)	.51* (22.19)	.97 (-1.65)	2184.56	948.
PACIFIC	3.25	.12 (1.17)	.68* (8.81)	.80** (-2.43)	73.06	141.
SOUTHERN	3.45	.53* (22.43)	.40* (23.64)	.94** (-3.77)	1791.59	2149.
WESTERN	2.70	.45* (14.45)	.54* (25.03)	.98 (-.72)	1075.25	1140.
THE UNITED STATES	2.52	.41* (29.98)	.56* (55.22)	.97** (-3.51)	6165.98	5565.

FOOTNOTES --
(1) THE COEFFICIENT IS COMPARED TO A VALUE OF ZERO FOR TESTS OF SIGNIFICANCE
(2) THE COEFFICIENT IS COMPARED TO A VALUE OF ONE FOR TESTS OF SIGNIFICANCE
* COEFFICIENT SIGNIFICANTLY GREATER THAN ZERO (ONE) AT THE FIVE PERCENT LEVEL
** COEFFICIENT SIGNIFICANTLY LESS THAN ZERO (ONE) AT THE FIVE PERCENT LEVEL
REGIONS NOT APPEARING ABOVE MET ONE OF TWO CONDITIONS . . .
 (1) SAMPLE SIZE SMALLER THAN TWELVE, OR
 (2) NO SAMPLE FOR THE REGION (SEE TABLE 3.1)
REGIONS AS DESCRIBED IN THE TEXT

With the exception (again) of the Pacific region the output elasticities are all rather similar to one another and would imply that, in 1850, labor's share of costs should have been in the range of 46 to 56 percent of total costs being lowest in the mid-West and highest in the South. On the basis of the national estimate, we would estimate the labor share of costs at 42 percent of the total. Estimates of factor shares made by Budd using different methods suggest that the factor share of labor in industry should be between 46.1 and 47.1 percent and that for the economy as a whole the share should be between 34.5 and 41.5 percent, closer to 41.5 percent than to the lower end of the range.[1] The estimates here are entirely consistent with and very close to these independent estimates.

The estimates of scale economies also serve to further emphasize the absence of any evidence warranting a claim of increasing returns in the South and constant returns elsewhere, especially in New England such as is implicit in the Russel-Linden-Genovese hypothesis.[2]

II. Census Year 1860

The manufacturing sector in all regions in 1860 was subject to either constant or increasing returns to scale as shown in Table 7.2. Only New England exhibited significantly increasing returns to scale suggesting that manufacturing enterprises were operating below capacity for their given plants. These results contrast quite sharply with those for 1850 where three of the regions, the Middle Atlantic states, the Pacific states and the South all had significantly decreasing returns to scale. The switch to constant, or marginally increasing returns to scale in the

TABLE 7.2

ORDINARY LEAST SQUARES ESTIMATES OF THE AGGREGATE PRODUCTION FUNCTION FOR EACH REGION
CENSUS YEAR 1860
(T-RATIO)

REGION	INTERCEPT TERM	COEFFICIENT OF LABOR CAPITAL (1) (1)	ECONOMIES OF SCALE (2)	F-RATIO	SAMPLE SIZE
MIDDLE ATLANTIC	2.93	.49* .50* (19.05) (24.27)	.99 (-.66)	2009.97	1129.
NEW ENGLAND	1.91	.42* .62* (14.39) (23.89)	1.04* (2.61)	2174.21	931.
PACIFIC	2.27	.39* .65* (6.82) (15.34)	1.04 (.90)	296.14	471.
SOUTHERN	2.94	.53* .49* (23.59) (28.58)	1.02 (1.47)	2524.10	1974.
WESTERN	2.96	.46* .50* (16.00) (25.29)	.97 (-1.58)	1397.69	1571.
THE UNITED STATES	2.59	.45* .55* (35.25) (55.51)	1.00 (-.18)	7920.01	6076.

FOOTNOTES --
(1) THE COEFFICIENT IS COMPARED TO A VALUE OF ZERO FOR TESTS OF SIGNIFICANCE
(2) THE COEFFICIENT IS COMPARED TO A VALUE OF ONE FOR TESTS OF SIGNIFICANCE
* COEFFICIENT SIGNIFICANTLY GREATER THAN ZERO (ONE) AT THE FIVE PERCENT LEVEL
** COEFFICIENT SIGNIFICANTLY LESS THAN ZERO (ONE) AT THE FIVE PERCENT LEVEL
REGIONS NOT APPEARING ABOVE MET ONE OF TWO CONDITIONS . . . .
    (1) SAMPLE SIZE SMALLER THAN TWELVE, OR
    (2) NO SAMPLE FOR THE REGION (SEE TABLE 3.1)
REGIONS AS DESCRIBED IN THE TEXT

South is a reflection of the expansion of southern plant and equipment and a more general increase in the number of manufacturing enterprises over the decade. At the same time the expansion of southern demand may have been less than anticipated. For example, over the decade 1850-1860, William Gregg's famous Graniteville Cotton Mill in South Carolina increased output by only $15,176 (or by 5.5 percent) despite an increase in capitalization of $50,000 (a 16.7 percent increase), although some of this increase in productive potential was offset by a labor force reduction of fourteen (or by 4 percent). Physical output increased over the decade by 161,318 yards of cotton sheeting, and price per yard remained constant at eight cents. Hence, the observed increase in output value exactly matches the increase in phyical output.[3] The increase in the capital-labor ratio implicit in these figures for William Gregg's factory reflected the general trend between 1850 and 1860 towards the use of less labor intensive methods and the substitution of capital for labor.

According to the output elasticities with respect to labor regional factor shares declined somewhat between 1850 and 1860 to a range of 38-52 percent of total cost being highest in the South once again and lowest in the New England and Pacific states. The national estimate implies that labor's share should have increased slightly to approximately 45 percent of total costs by 1860. This would be consistent with Budd's estimates of 45.1-45.4 percent for the share in industry but rather less than his estimate of 35.4-39.9 percent overall share.[4] These estimates, however, fall in the range defined by our results.

III. Census Year 1870

Missing data prevent the regional production function estimates for 1870 from being directly comparable with the estimates for 1850 and 1860. However, as Table 7.3 shows, at the regional level both the South and West as well as the nation as a whole had significantly decreasing returns to scale. Indeed the results look very similar to those for 1850. A ten percent increase in both labor and capital would be predicted to raise output by as little as 8.7 percent or by as much as 10.1 percent depending upon the region.

These results however conflict with factor share estimates made by Budd.[5] According to Budd, labor's share of factor payments rose between 1860 and 1870 from about 45 percent in industry to 49-50 percent by 1870 while the national share rose to 40-46.3 percent. Our estimates range on a regional level from 22-51 percent with only the estimates for the Middle Atlantic and New England states being even close to the estimates by Budd. Nationally our estimate of labor's share in manufacturing industry is 34 percent implying a considerable decline in labor's relative position over the Civil War decade compared with an improvement shown by Budd. The source of the discrepancy is unknown but it would seem that my estimates are too low while those of Budd are overly optimistic as the labor market begins to normalize after the scarcity of the Civil War years.

These results serve to reinforce the industry estimates presented in Chapters 5 and 6. The overwhelming weight of the evidence, particu-

TABLE 7.3

ORDINARY LEAST SQUARES ESTIMATES OF THE AGGREGATE PRODUCTION FUNCTION FOR EACH REGION
CENSUS YEAR 1870
(T-RATIO)

REGION	INTERCEPT TERM	COEFFICIENT OF LABOR (1)	COEFFICIENT OF CAPITAL (1)	ECONOMIES OF SCALE (2)	F-RATIO	SAMPLE SIZE
MIDDLE ATLANTIC	3.46	.49* (12.78)	.47* (16.35)	.96 (-1.71)	1098.06	555.
NEW ENGLAND	2.30	.42* (13.39)	.59* (23.10)	1.01 (.43)	2575.44	908.
PACIFIC	2.24	.33* (6.94)	.65* (17.86)	.97 (-.80)	560.68	357.
SOUTHERN	2.27	.33* (11.84)	.60* (31.23)	.93** (-3.33)	1458.54	2025.
WESTERN	1.91	.19* (5.97)	.68* (26.52)	.87** (-5.80)	990.70	634.
THE UNITED STATES	2.18	.32* (21.08)	.63* (54.98)	.95** (-5.01)	6335.73	4479.

FOOTNOTES --
(1) THE COEFFICIENT IS COMPARED TO A VALUE OF ZERO FOR TESTS OF SIGNIFICANCE
(2) THE COEFFICIENT IS COMPAPED TO A VALUE OF ONE FOR TESTS OF SIGNIFICANCE
* COEFFICIENT SIGNIFICANTLY GREATER THAN ZERO (ONE) AT THE FIVE PERCENT LEVEL
** COEFFICIENT SIGNIFICANTLY LESS THAN ZERO (ONE) AT THE FIVE PERCENT LEVEL
REGIONS NOT APPEARING ABOVE MET ONE OF TWO CONDITIONS . . .
  (1) SAMPLE SIZE SMALLER THAN TWELVE, OR
  (2) NO SAMPLE FOR THE REGION (SEE TABLE 3.1)
REGIONS AS DESCRIBED IN THE TEXT

larly in the production of inter-regionally traded commodities and for the aggregate production function, points to constant or decreasing returns to scale as characterizing the production conditions in each region and year. Assuming constant returns to scale, as many theoretical works do, bends the empirical evidence a little, but by no means as much as Genovese's claim of increasing returns to scale in the South and constant returns elsewhere.

CHAPTER 8

THE SENSITIVITY OF RETURNS TO SCALE TO UNITS AND METHODS OF MEASUREMENT

All estimates hitherto have been made on a consistent basis in order to facilitate comparisons. However, as indicated in Chapter 3, three fundamental assumptions have been made with respect to the data:

i) Capital services, including those of working capital are adequately measured by the reported capital investment (gross book value at original cost) plus an estimate for working capital derived from the ratio of working capital to output in Census year, 1890.

ii) Labor services may be estimated by an unweighted sum of employees as listed in the manuscript censuses, and

iii) Output may be measured by value-added.

Additionally, I have also implicitly assumed that even if the underlying production function was a CES function, there is no bias imparted to the returns to scale parameter estimated from an unconstrained Cobb-Douglas production function. As shown in Chapter 2 (Table 2.1) bias from this source is likely if and only if the elasticity of substitution is much different from unity.

These assumptions will be progressively relaxed in this chapter using data from southern lumber milling in 1850. This choice was essentially arbitrary except that the product is expected to be relatively homogeneous among firms, permitting aggregation of physical units. Sample size is also large. Since this industry did not employ a significant amount of female labor in any region, it has been supplemented by the sample data for the U.S. textiles industry.

I. Sensitivity to the Measurement of Capital

Assuming, for the moment, that the caiptal measure used hitherto is fundamentally correct, working capital estimates were adjusted by fifty percent in both directions. The resulting estimates, given in Table 8.1, reveal that although the relative magnitude of the coefficients of labor and capital change as the working capital is changed, the returns to scale parameter changes only marginally. In absolute terms, the mean dollar difference between the capital estimate with working capital reduced by fifty percent and that when working capital is increased by fifty percent is approximately $900. This change in capital represents about a thirty percent difference in the estimated capital between the low and the high estimates. Further, we note that as estimated capital increases, the magnitude of the capital coefficient also increases.[1]

Moving to an approximated measure of the flow of capital services, measured as the sum of estimated straight-line depreciation for the year,[2] insurance, maintenance and repair expenditures[3] and an interest charge of twenty-nine percent[4] on estimated working capital[5] results in a minor decrease in the returns to scale parameter. Amending the above estimate to include the opportunity cost of all capital services results in an increase in the returns to scale parameter to 1.15 or marginally above the estimate made with no changes.

Table 8.1

Sensitivity Analysis of Changes in the Measurement of Capital Services: Southern Lumber Milling, 1860
(t-ratio)

Production Function Form and Changes Made[1]	Labor	Coefficient of: Capital	$[Capital/Labor]^2$	Returns to Scale
I. Cobb-Douglas[2]				
a) No Changes	.60* (10.87)	.54* (11.54)	--	1.14* (4.26)
b) Working Capital Increased 50%	.51* (9.55)	.63* (13.83)	--	1.14* (4.43)
c) Working Capital Decreased 50%	.74* (13.04)	.41 (8.51)	--	1.15* (4.17)
d) Capital Services Measure[3]	.43* (8.92)	.70* (17.66)	--	1.13* (4.46)
e) Modified Capital Services Measure[3]	.67* (12.09)	.48* (10.15)	--	1.15* (4.35)
II. Kmenta's Approximation to the CES[2]				
a) No Changes	.50 (--)	.64 (1.08)	-.01 (-.17)	1.14 (4.24)
b) Working Capital Increased 50%	1.03 (--)	.11 (.18)	.04 (.89)	1.14* (4.47)
c) Working Capital Decreasing 50%	-.07 (--)	1.22* (2.11)	-.06 (-1.40)	1.15* (4.14)
d) Capital Services Measure[3]	1.45 (--)	-.31 (-.86)	.10* (2.79)	1.14* (4.79)
e) Modified Capital Services Measure[3]	.30 (--)	.85 (1.70)	-.03 (-.75)	1.15* (4.31)

[1] See text for description of the changes
[2] See Chapter 2 for the form of the equation
[3] See text for a description of this measure

*Significantly greater than zero (one, for returns to scale)
**Significantly less than zero (one, for returns to scale)

Between the five estimates made, mean capital varies from a low of $510 for my first approximated measure of the flow of capital services to a high of $3800 for the estimate with working capital increased by fifty percent. The F-ratio proved to be greatest for the capital servies measures indicating that this regression "explained" the greatest amount of total variation. A sufficient condition for such a result would be a diminution of the variability of the capital estimate, other things being equal. This, however, was not observed. Indeed, the variance of the capital estimate increased as a result of the change in the capital measure. On the other hand, the "worst" regression estimate proved to be that made with working capital reduced by fifty percent.

The pattern of the changes in the F-ratio is essentially that of the implied labor intensity of technique, with the most capital intensive technique having the lowest F-ratio. A switch in the production function form was noted. This switching of the forms of the production between those representing relatively low labor intensity techniques and those representing relatively high labor intensity techniques would lead us to conclude on the basis of the results and the F-ratios that the "true" underlying production function has a pronounced bias towards labor intensive techniques.

The CES estimates given in Table 8.1 are of interest on three counts. First, the estimate of the returns to scale parameter is almost invariant, differing by less than 0.01, between CES and Cobb-Douglas forms, supporting the Maddala and Kadane findings.[6] No appreciable bias in the returns to scale parameter results from the estimation of a Cobb-Douglas production function in preference to a CES production function. Second, in only one instance is the coefficient of the squared capital-labor ratio significantly different from zero suggesting that the elasticity of substitution between labor and capital differs from unity. In this particular case the estimate of the returns to scale parameter derived from the Cobb-Douglas differs from that derived from the CES function by .0095, the Cobb-Douglas estimate being the lower. Third, despite the addition of one extra variable in the regression equation, the CES production function performs less well in "explaining" total variablility estimate by estimate. Indeed, the general lack of significance among individual coefficients and the lack of conclusive evidence for an elasticity of substitution significantly different from unity would lead one to prefer the simpler Cobb-Douglas form.

The minor fluctuations in the returns to scale parameter for large changes in the capital measure are so slight as to cause little concern that inaccuracies in our principal measure of capital will lead to erroneous conclusions. Where significant economies of scale or diseconomies of scale have been found such changes would not alter the conclusions.

II. Sensitivity to the Measurement of Labor

As noted earlier, few industries in the nineteenth century employed significant quantities of female labor, and consequently, estimating labor input as a weighted sum of employees, where female labor is weighted by the ratio of the average female wage rate to the average male wage rate, required that a new industry be selected for the sensitivity analysis. Textile manufacturing was selected because of the high proportion of female employees. The principal sensitivity tests for variations in the labor measure are made with this industry for 1860. However, it was possible to make some limited adjustments to the labor measure for lumber milling. These are also reported in Table 8.2 together with the more detailed results for textile manufacturing.

Table 8.2

Sensitivity Analysis of Changes in the Measurement of Labor:
Textile Manufacturing 1860 and Southern Lumber Milling 1860
(t-ratio)

Production Function Form and Changes Made[1]	Labor	Coefficient of: Capital	[Capital/Labor][2]	Returns to Scale
I. Cobb-Douglas[2]				
A. Textiles				
a) No Changes	.29* (3.07)	.62* (6.28)	--	.91** (-2.27)
b) Unweighted Sum but including Employers	.27* (2.56)	.62* (6.28)	--	.90** (-2.41)
c) Weighted Sum including Employers	.23* (1.98)	.66* (6.52)	--	.90** (-2.25)
B. Lumber				
a) No Changes	.60* (10.87)	.54* (11.54)	--	1.14* (4.26)
b) Unweighted Sum but including Employers	.59* (9.38)	.58* (11.94)	--	1.18* (3.76)
II. Kmenta's Approximation to the CES				
A. Textiles				
a) No Changes	3.01 (--)	-2.11 (-1.48)	.19 (1.93)	.90** (2.58)
b) Unweighted Sum but including Employers	3.13 (--)	-2.25 (-1.59)	.20* (2.03)	.88 (-2.79)
c) Weighted Sum including Employers	4.45 (--)	-3.56 (-1.95)	.29* (2.40)	.89** (-2.61)
B. Lumber				
a) No Changes	.50 (--)	.64 (1.08)	-.01 (-.17)	1.14 (4.24)
b) Unweighted Sum but including Employers	.50 (--)	.68 (1.14)	-.01 (-.24)	1.18 (3.75)

Footnotes: See Table 8.1

For textiles manufacture the labor adjustments result in an increase in the man labor estimate from 24.5 employees for the original unweighted sum measure to 29 employee equivalents when an adjustment for managerial staff is made to the unweighted estimate. The weighted measure estimated labor to be 25 male employee equivalents. The estimate of the returns to scale parameter fell marginally by .016 when the unweighted sum was adjusted for the possible exclusion of supervisory and managerial personnel and fell by .013 when a weighted sum of employees was used. Such changes are, however, marginal. The addition of estimated managerial personnel to the unweighted sum proved to give the best fit in terms of the ability of the regression to "explain" total variability. However, an identical adjustment in lumber milling resulted in a less significant regression, but a much greater increase in the estimate of the returns to scale parameter. In this case, though the _significance_ of the returns to scale parameter decreased.

Clearly no single adjustment can be judged the "best" in terms of decreasing the relatively high degree of variability in the micro-data and hence, improving the fit of the regression equation.

Once again, the CES estimates of the returns to scale parameter parallelled those for the Cobb-Douglas, but for the textiles manufacture evidence of non-unitary elasticity of substitution of labor for capital was quite strong, although it does not result in appreciable bias in the returns to scale parameter.[7] The overall significance of the CES estimates, however, was much lower than that for the Cobb-Douglas while the negative coefficient for capital, though not quite significant at the five percent level, is cause for concern. This problem does not appear in the Cobb-Douglas estimates.

III. Sensitivity to the Measurement of Output

Changing the output measure for lumber milling from value-added to feet of lumber milled resulted in a significant change in the estimate of the returns to scale parameter, which fell from 1.14 showing significant increasing returns to scale to 1.05 at which level the hypothesis of constant returns to scale could not be rejected. The results are shown in Table 8.3.

Clearly the estimates of the returns to scale parameter made using value-added data as a proxy for physical output are biased vis a vis those estimates measuring physical data. This bias in the returns to scale parameter is significant. However, the crucial issue is not bias, since this must unfortunately be a natural consequence of our inability to estimate most production functions using any other measure. The crucial issue is therefore whether or not the bias is consistent.

In an attempt to resolve this issue, estimates for lumber milling and flour milling in each regions were made using both measures of output. Unfortunately, as a comparison of the estimates of the returns to scale parameter quickly revealed, the bias was not consistent either with respect to magnitude or sign. Of the twenty-three comparisons made, the estimate of the returns to scale parameter made using value data is greater than the corresponding estimate made using quantity data in fourteen instances, ten of which are for lumber milling, while the magnitude of the differential between the estimates varies from a low of .01 for Western flour milling in 1860 to a high of .41 for New England flour milling in 1860.

Even more disturbing than the lack of consistency in the bias is the frequency with which conclusions are changed. Ten of the twenty-three

Table 8.3

Sensitivity of the Returns to Scale Parameter to Changes
in the Measurement of Output:
Southern Lumber Milling 1860

Production Function Form and Changes made[1]	Labor	Coefficient of: Capital	[Capital/Labor][2]	Returns to Scale
A. Cobb-Douglas[2]				
a) Value data	.60* (10.87)	.54* (11.54)	--	1.14* (4.26)
b) Physical data	.67* (11.89)	.38* (7.65)	--	1.05 (1.50)
B. Kmenta's Approximation[2] to the CES				
a) Value data	.50 (--)	.64 (1.08)	-.01 (-.17)	1.14* (4.24)
b) Physical Data	-.94 (--)	1.99* (3.26)	-.12** (-2.64)	1.05 (1.36)

Footnotes: See Table 8.1

conclusions arrived at using value data would be changed on the basis of the quantity data estimates, and in the case of United States lumber milling in 1850 diametrically opposed conclusions would be reached.

However, three factors weaken these conclusions. First, in only two instances did quantity data outperform value data in explaining total variability in the micro-data. Second, sample sizes for quantity data were always smaller than those for value data raising the question of the degree of reliability and consistency in the reporting of quantity data. Third, the problem of quantity and product differentials remains unanswered. Indeed, this latter criticism is serious. As previously noted most firms even among these two homogeneous industries produced more than one product or grade of product. In particular, I have assumed that a bushel of milled grain is a homogeneous product. Since most flour mills in the South produced both flour and corn meal, while those elsewhere produced flour, corn meal, buckwheat and rye, homogeneity cannot be asserted. Price, whether it primarily reflects quality differences, market differentials or more fundamental product differentials, is an important factor and the overriding consideration in this work is to assess the performance and adaptation of nineteenth century firms in the field of production to their markets. Price, therefore, cannot be ignored and value-added data remains the only value-free method of measuring the contributions of organized factors of production to the creation of utility and satisfaction of human wants.

On the basis of these results it seems reasonable to conclude that even fairly large changes in the measurement of either the labor input or the capital input have minimal effect upon the magnitude of the returns to scale parameter. Changes in the measurement of labor or capital inputs change the relative magnitudes of the output elasticities, but not to a significant extent. However, serious and inconsistent bias may be present in the results due to the use of value-added data as a proxy for physical output measures. Short of discarding most of the data and confining attention to a very limited subset of the data, no solution to this problem is possible.

CHAPTER 9

SOME EVIDENCE ON DECREASING SCALE ELASTICITY

The three production function forms developed by Nerlove[1] Ringstad[2] and Zellner and Revankar[3] have the property that as output increases, the estimated scale elasticity decreases. Such a property corresponds to the assumed behavior of economies of size in economic theory and the returns to scale parameter as identified with the assumed U-shape of the long-run average cost curve. Each form behaves similarly, although the results obtained by Ringstad suggest that each form leads to a marginally different estimate of the magnitude of the returns to scale parameter when evaluated at the same output level.[4]

Consider the production function form developed by Zellner and Revankar:

$$\log V + \Theta V = \mu \log L + \beta \log \frac{K}{L} \qquad [9.1]$$

which has scale elasticity of:

$$\varepsilon = \mu/(1 + \Theta \cdot V) \qquad [9.2]$$

which depends upon the two parameters μ and Θ and upon the level of output (in this case measured by value-added) selected.

For the i-th firm, this production function may be written as

$$\log (V^\lambda)_i = \mu \cdot \log L_i + \beta \cdot \log \frac{K_i}{L_i} + u_i \qquad [9.3]$$

where $\log (V^\lambda)_i = \log V_i + \Theta V_i$, a monotonic transformation of V_i and u_i is the random ("Acts of God") disturbance term assumed to be normally and independently distributed with mean zero and variance of σ^2.

The direct least squares estimation of equation [9.3] for some predetermined value of θ will provide an estimate of μ and hence of the returns to scale parameter. But there are an infinite number of values of θ possible under this criterion and little confidence can be attached to the resultant estimate of the returns to scale parameter.

However, a non-linear maximum likelihood estimator similar to that suggested by Box and Cox,[5] provides a consistent estimation technique. The logarithm of the likelihood function corresponding to [9.3] is:

$$\log \ell = \text{constant} - \frac{n}{2} \log \sigma^2 + \log J(\lambda;V)$$

$$- \frac{1}{2\sigma^2} \sum_{i=1}^{n} [\log (V^\lambda)_i - \mu \cdot \log L_i - \beta \cdot \log \frac{K_i}{L_i}]^2 \quad [9.4]$$

where constant $= -(n/2)\log 2\pi$, σ^2 is as defined below, n is the number of observations and $J(\lambda;V)$ is the Jacobian of the monotonic transformation, $J(\lambda;V) = \prod_{i=1}^{n} \frac{d \log(V\lambda)}{d \log V}$. But $\log(V^\lambda) = \log V + \theta V$ in this particular instance and hence the Jacobian reduces to

$$J(\lambda;V) = \prod_{i=1}^{n} (1 + \theta V_i) = \sum_{i=1}^{n} \log(1 + \theta V_i)$$

The Jacobians for the Nerlove and the Ringstad transformations may be similarly determined.[6]

The likelihood function is therefore

$$\log \ell = \text{constant} - \frac{n}{2} \log \sigma^2 + \sum_{i=1}^{n} \log(1 + \theta V_i)$$

$$- \frac{1}{2\sigma^2} \sum_{i=1}^{n} (\log V_i + \theta V_i - \mu \cdot \log L_i - \beta \cdot \log \frac{K_i}{L_i})^2 \quad [9.5]$$

In [9.5], notice that the least squares criterion minimizes

$$\sum_{i=1}^{n} [\log V_i + \Theta V_i - \mu \cdot \log L_i - \beta \cdot \log \frac{K_i}{L_i}]^2 \qquad [9.6]$$

for any given value of Θ. Hence, for any given value of Θ, the ordinary least squares regression

$$\log(V^\lambda)_i = \mu \cdot \log L_i + \beta \cdot \log \frac{K_i}{L_i} + u_i$$

will maximize the likelihood function [9.5] for that given value of Θ. By varying Θ and observing the resultant value of the likelihood function, the global maximum of the likelihood function may be determined. Evaluating [9.5] for various values of Θ is tedious but the expression may be simplified. Differentiating equation [9.5] with respect to σ^2 gives:

$$\frac{\partial \log \ell}{\partial \sigma^2} = -\frac{n}{2\sigma^2} + \frac{1}{2(\sigma^2)^2} \sum_{i=1}^{n} [\log(V^\lambda)_i - \mu \log L_i - \beta \log \frac{K_i}{L_i}]^2 \qquad [9.7]$$

and setting the partial [9.7] equal to zero gives

$$\frac{n}{2\sigma^2} = \frac{1}{2(\sigma^2)^2} \sum_{i=1}^{n} [\log(V^\lambda)_i - \mu \log L_i - \beta \log \frac{K_i}{L_i}]^2$$

reducing to:

$$n = \frac{1}{\hat{\sigma}^2} \sum_{i=1}^{n} [\log(V^\lambda)_i - \mu \log L_i - \beta \log \frac{K_i}{L_i}]^2$$

or:

$$\hat{\sigma}^2 = \frac{1}{n} \sum_{i=1}^{n} [\log(V^\lambda)_i - \mu \log L_i - \beta \log \frac{K_i}{L_i}]^2 \qquad [9.8]$$

as the conditional maximum for σ^2.

Equating $\hat{\sigma}^2$ to σ^2 and substituting [9.8] into [9.5] gives

$$\log \ell^* = \text{constant} - \frac{n}{2} \log \frac{1}{n} \sum_{i=1}^{n} [\log(V^\lambda)_i - \mu \log L_i - \beta \log \frac{K_i}{L_i}]^2$$

$$+ \sum_{i=1}^{n} \log(1 + \Theta V_i) \qquad [9.9]$$

Clearly in this formulation, given Θ, the regression [9.3] will result in a conditional maximum for the likelihood function for the predetermined value of Θ. By varying Θ and evaluating ($\log \ell^*$ - constant) the global maximum of the likelihood function can be determined.[7]

However, $\hat{\sigma}^2$ is a <u>biased</u> estimate of σ^2.[8] The best unbiased estimator of σ^2 is

$$s^2 = \frac{n}{(n-2)} \hat{\sigma}^2 = \frac{1}{(n-2)} \sum_{i=1}^{n} [\log(V^\lambda)_i - \mu \log L_i - \beta \log \frac{K_i}{L_i}]^2 \qquad [9.10]$$

If s^2 is now an unbiased estimate of σ^2 (8.10) is substituted in [8.5] we have

$$\log \ell^* = \text{constant} - \frac{n}{2} \log \frac{1}{n-2} \sum_{i=1}^{n} [\log(V^\lambda)_i - \mu \log L_i - \beta \log \frac{K_i}{L_i}]^2$$

$$+ \sum_{i=1}^{n} \log(1 + \Theta V_i) \qquad [9.11]$$

which is now an unbiased esitmate of the maximum of the likelihood function. We may then proceed as before, evaluating the conditional maxima ($\log \ell^*$ - constant), for given values of Θ until the global maximum is determined.

Using numerical methods, however, it is generally impractical and infeasible to determine the precise global maximum of the likelihood function due to the speed of convergence in the neighborhood of that maximum. In practice, therefore, one relies upon some terminal condition in the neighborhood of the maximum. For a very small step size, $\Delta\Theta$ (generally of the order of 10×10^{-6} or less), the algorithm selects the last value of Θ that resulted in an increase in the likelihood function as the estimate of Θ that maximizes the function. The maximum theoretical error in Θ is therefore $\Delta\Theta$, but will in general be much smaller.

A plot of $(\log \hat{\ell} - \log \hat{\ell}_{max})$ for southern flour mills in 1850 is shown in Figure 9.1. The distribution $(\log \hat{\ell} - \log \hat{\ell}_{max})$ follows the χ^2 distribution such that

$$(\log \hat{\ell} - \log \hat{\ell}_{max}) < \frac{1}{2} \chi^2_{\lambda\eta}$$

where λ is the number of independent components in the transformation ($\lambda=1$ for the Nerlove or Zellner and Revankar form and $\lambda=2$ for the Ringstad transformation) and η is the significance level.[9] For the Zellner and Revankar transformation the 95 percent confidence interval is defined by

$$(\log \hat{\ell} - \log \hat{\ell}_{max}) > -1.94$$

as shown in Figure 9.1.

Unless otherwise noted, the results presented here were made using the Zellner and Revankar transformation. Looking back at equation 9.2 we should recognize the implied constraint that:

$$1 + \Theta \cdot V > 0$$

or $$\Theta > -\frac{1}{V_{max}}$$

At the same time if scale elasticity, ϵ, is to decline with increasing value-added (output) then $\Theta > 0$. This restriction is not a necessary

Figure 9.1
Plot of $(\log \hat{\ell} - \log \hat{\ell}_{max})$ for Southern Flour Milling in 1850

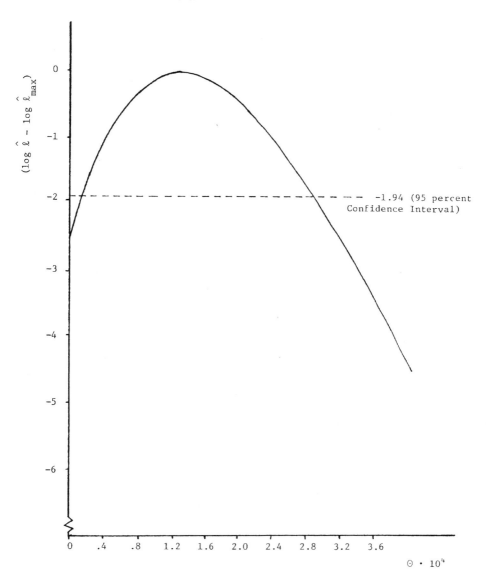

condition to estimate the likelihood function but rather is sufficient to ensure that scale elasticity is decreasing. For $0 > \theta > -\frac{1}{V_{max}}$ scale elasticity is increasing with value-added rather than decreasing. This result conflicts with economic theory and with the well-established proposition of a U-shaped (or a J- or an L-shaped) average cost curve. It implies, among other things, that average costs are monotonically decreasing and that the optimal plant size is one that, in the absence of positive transport or other distribution costs or externalities, supplies the entire market. The existence of such costs, however, imposes an upper limit on plant size. As we shall see below, this observation is important.

I. Intra-Regionally Traded Commodities.

Table 9.1 presents the best estimates of the variable scale elasticity production function for 1850, 1860 and 1870 for the intra-regionally traded commodities, lumber and flour. Scale elasticity is variable as value-added, V, varies and is defined by:

$$\varepsilon = \mu/(1 + \theta V)$$

as shown in equation [9.2]. The evidence does not point to particularly variable scale elasticity for these two products as the parameter θ is only significantly positive in two cases: southern flour milling in 1850 and flour milling in New England in 1870. Moreover, in a number of cases we were forced to widen the search for the maximum of the likelihood function to include negative values of θ. None proved to be significantly negative, but negative values of θ occurred about as frequently

TABLE 9.1

VARIABLE SCALE ELASTICITY PRODUCTION FUNCTION ESTIMATES FOR REGIONALLY TRADED COMMODITIES, 1850-1870

Industry and Region	1850 μ	1850 $10^4\theta$	1860 μ	1860 $10^4\theta$	1870 μ	1870 $10^4\theta$
Flour Milling						
Middle Atlantic	1.070	.077	1.057	-.029	1.374[b]	.019[d]
New England	1.184	-.500	1.076	-.071	1.299[b]	.095[d]
Pacific	.195[a]	.074[d]	1.306[b]	.052	.778	-.057
Southern	1.672[b]	1.331[d]	1.382[b]	.014	1.017[b]	-.124
Mid-West	1.066	-.016	1.194	.024	1.514[b]	.278
Lumber Milling						
Middle Atlantic	.862[a]	-.202	1.217[b]	.041	1.188	.411
New England	.954[b]	-.081	1.059[b]	-.010	1.106	-.001
Pacific	1.333[b]	.040	1.324[b]	.089	1.136[b]	.112
Southern	1.111[b]	-.081	1.142[b]	.002	1.275[b]	.029
Mid-West	1.351[b]	1.120	1.164[b]	.014	1.065	.083

[a] Significantly less than one at the five percent level

[b] Significantly greater than one at the five percent level

[c] Significantly less than zero at the five percent level

[d] Significantly greater than zero at the five percent level

Scale elasticity = $\mu/(1 + \theta \cdot V)$, where V is value-added.

as positive Θ. This suggests that the occurrence of negative Θ may be random. Indeed, that of course is what a result implies when a hypothesis (in this case H_o: Θ = 0) is not rejected.

Negative values for Θ imply somewhat unusual cost curve behavior and it seems worthwhile that we depict the shape of the implicit average cost curve for various combinations of μ and Θ. These characteristics are given in Table 9.2.

If those instances in which Θ was estimated to be negative are to be given serious consideration, then one must ask about the source of conditions that would cause cost to decrease at an increasing rate as plant size gets larger. Elsewhere I have suggested that this may be attributable to unidentified cost curve shifts to lower and lower costs as the plant gets larger and larger.[10] This would be consistent with the existence of external economies that were only available to larger plants on a discontinuous basis, for example, if there existed a threshold size before one could break through to take advantage of those externalities. The theory of this is not well developed and it is not my intention to attempt to develop it here.

More than half of the estimates of μ in Table 9.1 are significantly greater than unity and in all but one case (southern lumber milling in 1850) Θ was estimated to be positive (significantly so in two instances). In these instances then the evidence points to a U-shaped long-run average cost curve that exhibits the economies of scale behavior traditionally ascribed it. Figures 9.2 and 9.3 graph the variation in returns to scale with plant size for southern flour mills in 1850 and for flour mills in

TABLE 9.2

THE IMPLIED SHAPE OF THE LONG-RUN AVERAGE COST CURVE FROM
ELASTICITY PRODUCTION FUNCTION ESTIMATES[a]

Value of Θ	Value of μ	Implied Shape of LRAC
$\Theta > 0$	$\mu > 1$	U-shaped
	$\mu \leq 1$	J-shaped
$\Theta = 0$	$\mu > 1$	Monotronically decreasing
	$\mu = 1$	Constant
	$\mu < 1$	Monotronically increasing
$0 > \Theta > -1$	$\mu \geq 1$	Inverted J-shape
	$\mu < 1$	Inverted U-shape

[a] From the Zellner-Revankar generalized production function:

$$\ln V + \Theta V = \mu \ln L + \beta \ln\left(\frac{K}{L}\right).$$

Figure 9.2

Variable Scale Elasticity with Value-Added in Flour Milling in the
Southern States in 1850

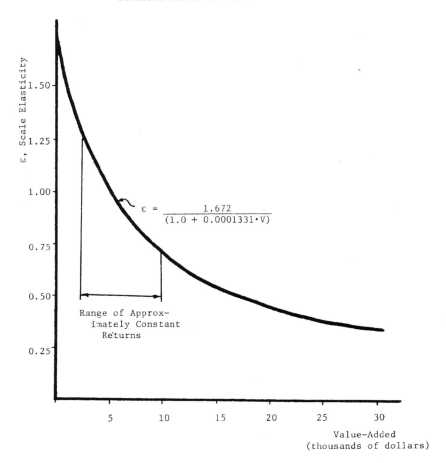

Figure 9.3

Variable Scale Elasticity with Value-Added in Flour Milling in
the Middle Atlantic States
1850

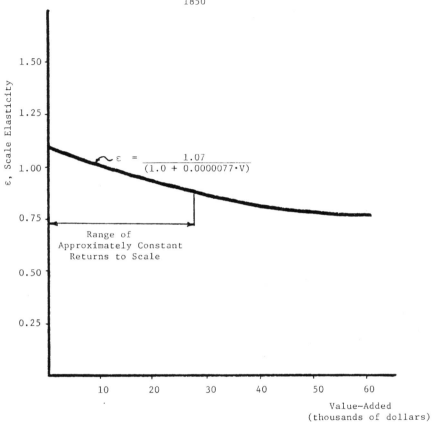

the Middle Atlantic states in 1850. In this latter instance μ was not significantly different from unity nor was Θ significantly different from zero.

In both Figure 9.2 and Figure 9.3, the range of plant sizes over which the hypothesis of constant returns to scale (and hence constant costs) cannot be rejected is clearly marked. For southern flour mills in 1850, plants in this range of approximately constant returns to scale produced almost 70 percent of the total industry value-added. In the Middle Atlantic states plants in this (much wider) range produced about 73 percent of the industry value-added. This kind of pattern appears to be quite typical.[11]

II. Inter-Regionally Traded Commodities

The decreasing scale elasticity estimates for the inter-regionally traded comodities are given in Table 9.3. Three things are notable about these results especially when they are compared with the estimates in Table 9.1. First, relatively few of the estimates of μ in Table 9.3 are significantly different from unity implying that the smallest plants in these industries were apparently able to realize all scale economies and produce under conditions of instant returns and constant costs. In only four instances was μ significantly different from unity and in each case it was significantly greater. Second, only seven of the estimates of Θ were negative. None was significantly so. As noted above this would therefore suggest that the typical average cost curve had a normal U- or J-shape in each industry in each region. Third, only one estimate of Θ was significantly positive indicating that the evidence favoring

TABLE 9.3

VARIABLE SCALE ELASTICITY PRODUCTION FUNCTION ESTIMATES FOR
INTER-REGIONALLY TRADED COMMODITIES, 1850-1870

Industry and Region	1850 μ	1850 $10^4\theta$	1860 μ	1860 $10^4\theta$	1870 μ	1870 $10^4\theta$
Boots and Shoes						
Middle Atlantic	1.017	.294	1.048	.095	1.048	.251
New England	.983	.008	.933	-.012	1.008	.023
Pacific	n.a.	n.a.	1.662[b]	1.726	1.039	-.091
South	.981	.337	1.132[b]	.906	1.088	.032
Mid-West	1.126	.278	1.273[b]	1.057	.977	.278
Clothing						
Middle Atlantic	1.036[b]	-.024[d]	.910	-.004	1.167	.134
New England	2.635[b]	4.404[d]	1.136	.065	.992	.014
Pacific	n.a.	n.a.	n.a.	n.a.	1.002	.047
South	.981	.166	.775	.026	1.012	.000
Mid-West	.938	.182	.775	-.231	.895	.005
Cotton Textiles						
Middle Atlantic	n.a.	n.a.	.864	-.006	n.a.	n.a.
New England	1.007	.241	.937	-.005	n.a.	n.a.
South	.756	.005	.741	.018	n.a.	n.a.

Footnotes: See Table 9.1

variable scale elasticity over constant scale elasticity production function estimates is rather weak.

In the foregoing discussion, little has been said about the historical implications of these estimates. It is to that topic I now turn. As noted above the production function estimates in chapters 5, 6 and 7 only provide evidence on what I called (in chapter 1) the third assumption of the Russel-Linden-Genovese hypothesis, namely that southern firms typically produced under conditions of increasing returns to scale and decreasing unit costs while northern enterprises produced under conditions of constant returns to scale and constant unit costs having exploited all potential scale economies. No basis for this was found. Those estimates, however, cast no light upon the first two assumptions that there existed substantial returns to scale over some range of outputs and that large plant sizes were necessary if these scale economies were to be realized. The estimates presented here generally contradict both claims.

The failure of the estimates of μ to be significantly greater than unity, especially in the production of inter-regionally traded commodities, denies the validity of the first assumption. In these instances in which μ was significantly greater than zero, however, scale elasticity declined (generally) quite sharply exhausting all scale economies at low levels of output. Indeed as Figures 9.2 and 9.3 indicate, not only is the range of increasing returns to scale rapidly exhausted but also that decreasing returns to scale set in at fairly low levels of value-added. This then denies that large size is nessary to realize scale economies.

Notwithstanding these conclusions, however, there is also evidence that production conditions differed quite sharply between small and large plants. If the data were divided into mutually exclusive groups of "small" and "large" plants and the estimates in Tables 9.1 and 9.3 repeated for each group then it would be found that for the "small" plants, μ was significantly greater than unity and Θ was significantly greater than zero, while for the "large" plants, μ was significantly less than unity and Θ was often significantly negative.[12]

This result is interpreted as indicating that there may be unidentified cost curve shifts for larger plants which were able to realize some advantages not available to the smaller plants such as preferential access to capital, superior management and so on.[13] The precise nature and extent of these, however, remains unknown. Moreover, these advantages may have been greater or more pronounced in the New England and Middle Atlantic states. Some more light is cast upon this problem in chapter 10 below. It should also be noted that these results, other than the feature of variable scale elasticity (no matter how slight), are quite similar to those presented earlier on the basis of the regular Cobb-Douglas production function.

Chapter 10

THE SURVIVOR TECHNIQUE AND OPTIMAL PLANT SIZE*

The survivor technique seeks to identify that size class or those classes of plant that not only survived the rigors of market competition and the test of time, but also succeeded in increasing their share of total industry value-added.[1] That is, it seeks to identify those plant sizes that grew in relative importance in an industry through the long-run competitive adjustment process.

A number of assumptions are implicit. The time span between observations must be sufficiently lengthy to permit long-run scale adjustments and for a clear, i.e., non-random, pattern to emerge. The long-run average cost curve is assumed to be stable, thereby precluding major technological advances and non-constant cost industries. Finally, all firms are operated by profit maximizing enterpreneurs. Shepherd argues that the survivor technique results are more likely to be valid for atomistically competitive industries than for highly concentrated ones, since in the former case, these assumptions insure that in the long-run, market pressures force all plants to operate at minimum long- and short-run average cost if they are to survive.[2] However, profit maximizing behavior also insures the survival of the lower cost plants even under conditions of monopolistic competition.[3] Under conditions of atomistic competition, price deviations about minimum long-run average cost are temporary and shifts in demand

---

*An earlier draft of this chapter was presented at the Western Social Sciences Association Conference, Denver, May 1975. See Bateman and Atack (1975) and Atack and Bateman (1977).

always induce compensatory changes in the number of plants in the industry, leaving the optimal plant size unchanged. On the other hand, in monopolistically competitive industries such changes will permanently alter the market solution including the optimum plant size.

If these conditions are satisfied then the survivor technique results may be generalized to one of four cases. Results showing a single size class of plants gaining in relative importance suggest a U-shaped long-run average cost curve and a determinate optimal plant size. The persistence of a wide range of size categories with no gainers but with some plants declining in relative importance at the limit(s) of the size spectrum suggests the presence of constant returns to scale over a wide range of outputs and hence of a relatively flat long-run average cost curve. When there are neither clear gainers or losers, optimal plant size is indeterminate and the long-run average cost curve horizontal. Lastly, if the largest size class is open-ended and is the only one growing in relative importance, then while it is impossible to specify the range of constant cost and constant returns to scale, one can specify the range where plants are sub-optimal and average costs are declining. Any of these results would be consistent with existing empirical cost function studies.[4]

The advantages, drawbacks and limitations inherent in the survivor technique have been discussed in detail by other users, particularly Shepherd,[5] but its most commonly-cited advantage--the ability to analyse changes in plant size over long time spans rather than in a purely static context--is worth emphasizing. Application of the survivor method further "finesses the problem of the capitalizaton of rents into costs, a process which drives disparate measured average costs towards equality"[6] which formed the core of Friedman's critique of cost function studies.[7] There are several recognized limitations. Social costs, for example, are not captured by the technique. Moreover, it may embrace other effects, such as externalities or technological change, which could lead to false impressions regarding internal scale economies.

Much of the debate over the survivor technique has been sparked by a failure of existing studies to satisfy the underlying assumptions and to provide an answer to William Shepherd's question, "What Does the Survivor Technique Show About Economies of Scale?"[8] rather than by the contradiction of its predictions. Failure to satisfy the assumptions may lead to bias in the survivor technique results. However, though it is generally impossible to correct the bias statistically because of the heuristic nature of the survivor algorithm, in many instances the nature of the potential bias may be specified a priori and hence taken into account.

Consider, for example, the nature of the bias arising from the existence of monopoly elements. Under conditions of monopolistic competition, long-run equilibrium is reached at some output less than that which minimized long-run average cost. Weiss[9] avoids this problem by emphasizing the "minimum efficient" scale of operation rather than the range of optimal plant sizes emphasized by others.[10] However, if surviving firms continue to be identified with minimum long-run average cost then the results will not only be biased but will also be inconsistent with production or cost function estimates which would show increasing returns to scale or decreasing unit costs.[11] Similarly, the presence of externalities which alter the cost minimizing level of output will lead to inconsistent results between the survivor technique or cost function estimates and those based upon production functions.

Alternate measures of plant size can yield quite different conclusions during periods of technological change. Ignoring the problems caused by shifts in the long-run average cost curve, let us assume that the survivor technique assumptions are satisfied, that the industry production function is consistent with a U-shaped long-run average cost curve[12] and that the technological change is such that the relationship between scale elasticity and output is unchanged. Under these circumstances, if plant size is measured by labor or capital, the survivor technique will show small plants surviving because of the shift of the isoquants towards the origin, while on an output basis, the optimal (or minimum efficient) plant size would be unchanged. Furthermore, if the technological change is labor-saving, then the apparent reduction in the size of the optimal plant will be greater if size is measured by employment rather than by capital and vice versa if the technological change is capital-saving.

Most empirical work has to confront the problem of random noise in the data, but tests of statistical significance permit one to correct for it and to specify a priori the confidence that one will have in the resultant estimates. Unfortunately such tests are not possible with the survivor technique, but the problems posed by the existence of random noise are most acute when the number of observations is small as is common with this approach. Because most survivor technique studies, with the exception of that by Shepherd, have used observations of the distribution of plant sizes at only two points in time, there is a higher probability that their results will be subject to random error.

1. Application of the Technique to Nineteenth Century Data

The manuscript censuses for 1850, 1860 and 1870 provide precisely the plant data required for the application of the survivor technique and the problems raised by twentieth century disclosure laws do not exist.

The survivor technique depends crucially upon the number of size categories and size classifications selected. The actual size categories selected are shown in Table 10.1. Increasing the number of size categories led to less dense matrices and the number of categories with no observations tended to confuse and obscure the results despite the large sample size in excess of 16,000 for all three census years. Varying the size limits while keeping ten size categories gave essentially similar results as might be expected.

Selection of the appropriate size classification--value-added, capital assets or employment--was determined by two considerations. While the literature on the survivor technique is not consistent in its selection of one size criterion in preference to the alternatives, there is general agreement in favor of the use of the value-added criterion, but actual use of this criterion for the twentieth century is limited by disclosure laws. Furthermore, as noted in Chapter 3, the data in respect of both capital and labor are considered somewhat less reliable than the data on input and output values. The capital estimates are probably the least reliable statistic in the manuscript censuses, while the possible incomplete reporting of _all_ labor inputs including proprietorship would unduly bias the results for small firms.

Table 10.1

Size Categories

Size Code	Value-Added ($)
A	0 - 100
B	101 - 500
C	501 - 1,000
D	1,001 - 2,000
E	2,001 - 5,000
F	5,001 - 10,000
G	10,001 - 20,000
H	20,001 - 30,000
I	30,001 - 50,000
J	50,001 - 100,000

A. Regional Overview, 1850 - 1870.

Table 10.2 offers a regional overview of the survival of plants in all industries for the period 1850 - 1870. Surviving and minimum efficient plant sizes are coded as shown in Table 10.1.

The results are classified into three groups. Results identified as "clear" represent one or more clearly defined adjacent size categories gaining in their relative contribution to total value-added in each of the three census years. Those classified as "unclear" have one or more adjacent size categories gaining in their relative contributions to total value-added from 1850 to 1870 while their contribution declined in 1860. Finally those results identified as "inconsistent" showed two or more non-adjacent size categories simultaneously gaining in their relative contributions to total value-added. This latter result is inconsistent with a uni-modal long-run average cost curve and is discussed in greater detail below.

Results for the Middle Atlantic states were unclear. The $50,000-$100,000 size category showed a two percent decline it its contribution to total value-added between 1850 and 1860, but increased its relative contribution by .3% over the whole period. The production function estimates for the Middle Atlantic states indicated that while in 1850, these states had produced under decreasing returns to scale, constant returns to scale prevailed in 1860 and 1870. However, the decreasing scale elasticity estimates given in Chapter 9 would indicate that these plants were subject to significant diseconomies of scale with scale elasticity of the order of .75 in 1860. The apparent conflict between the results arises because under ideal circumstances the estimates measure different factors. The

Table 10.2

Optimal Size Categories of Plant and Minimum Efficient
Plant Size by Region 1850-1870

Region	Optimal Plant Size	Percentage of Total Value-Added Produced in Optimally Sized Plants 1850	Percentage of Total Value-Added Produced in Optimally Sized Plants 1870	Minimum Efficient Plant Size	Status
Middle Atlantic	I,J	23.6	64.7	I	Unclear
New England	I,J	18.0	66.1	I	Clear
Pacific	J	9.7	55.0	J	Clear
South	A-D	26.6	29.6	A	Unclear
West	J	0.0	31.3	J	Clear
United States	I,J	22.9	52.8	I	Clear

production function estimates should reflect only factors internal to the firm, while the survivor technique captures both internal and external economies. The decreasing scale elasticity estimates imply that, at constant factor prices, average cost in the optimal size categories indentified by the survivor technique would be approximately 14% higher than the average cost in a plant of size $10,000, where scale elasticity was approximately unity.[13]

On this basis, therefore, the entrepreneurial decision to build the larger plant was an unwise decision. By definition, ex ante the entrepreneur can have little or no knowledge about the magnitude of external economies, otherwise these external economies could be internalized by the firm. However, at the same time the entrepreneur probably had some expectations at least with respect to the direction of potential external economies. Ex post these expectations may or may not be realized. Given the ex post situation in which the entrepreneur found himself, the presence and magnitude of external economies of scale may have saved him from the consequences of his poor ex ante judgment. This 14% margin should therefore represent the minimum reduction in external costs necessary to persuade an entrepreneur to keep his resources in a plant of this size.

Since at best, external economy margins are unknown to the entrepreneur ex ante, building this optimal size plant is a trial-and-error proposition and the result of fortuitous circumstances. As table 10.2 shows, by 1870, these large optimally sized plants in the Middle Atlantic states accounted for over sixty percent of manufacturing value-added.

Results for New England showed a clear trend towards production in large scale plants producing more than $50,000 value-added. Such plants by 1870 accounted for over sixty-five percent of New England's manufacturing value-added, up from only eighteen percent in 1850. Aggregate production function estimates for New England showed constant returns to scale in each census year, while the decreasing scale elasticity estimates closely approximated those for the Middle Atlantic states. These results once again suggest that external economies of scale, not captured in my production function estimates, may have reduced average costs in these large scale plants by approximately 14%.

The surviving size category of firms in the Pacific states was also clearly defined to be that producing in excess of $100,000 value-added per year, which by 1870 accounted for fifty-five percent of manufacturing value-added in California and Oregon. The decreasing scale elasticity estimates suggest that for such plants to be the rational choice of a profit maximizing entrepreneur they must have been able to secure external economies in excess of twenty percent since both decreasing scale elasticity estimates suggest that such plants would have returns to scale parameter of the order of .60 as an upper bound.

Results for the South were unclear, but suggest that the optimal plant size in the South was no larger than $2,000. In conjunction with the decreasing scale elasticity estimates of Chapter 9 which show increasing returns to scale over this range of the order 1.05-1.20, this result suggests the presence of substantial external diseconomies of scale in South, raising average costs by between three and ten percent. Regular production function estimates for the South also showed significant decreasing returns to scale in both 1850 and 1870. The survivor technique result reinforces that conclusion but leaves unanswered the important question of the source of these apparent external diseconomies. The presence of substantial external diseconomies would also explain the slow rate of growth of these "optimally" sized plants over the period, which increased their share of value-added by only 3%. Since the status of the results for the South was unclear, however, the overall significance of these results must be downgraded.

Results for the western region showed a clear gain in the manufacturing value-added produced by the largest-sized plants. No such plants had existed in 1850, yet by 1870 these plants produced almost one-third of the western region's manufacturing value-added. The lack of any sample for Illinois in 1850 probably accounts for the absence of any such plants in 1850, while it is likely that had Missouri been available in 1870 the contribution by such plants would probably have been greater. According to the decreasing scale elasticity estimates such plant should have had substantial decreasing returns to scale in production of between .90 and .40. The persistence and growth of this size of plant therefore, implies substantial external economies of scale reducing average costs by between five and forty-three percent.

In the light of these results, it is not surprising that for the nation as a whole the large plants producing in excess of $50,000 value-added survived and apparently prospered. By 1870 more than one-half of the nation's manufacturing value-added was produced by such plants. Since the regular production function estimates indicated significant decreasing returns to scale in production in both 1850 and 1870, the results once again imply the presence of substantial external economies, a proposition that makes sense both historically and theoretically.

The documentary evidence is replete with examples of external economies that accrued especially to firms in the more developed (i.e. New England

and Middle Atlantic states) areas of the country. For example specialization was more pronounced in New England than elsewhere. In cotton manufacture, the Rhode Island mills produced finer grade cloths than those of Massachusetts[14] while in Masachusetts the boot and shoe industry was distinguished by the specialization between towns, Lynn in the manufacture of women's shoes, Danvers in children's shoes and Marlboro in men's footwear.[15]

The change in the percentage of value-added produced in optimally sized plants may be taken as a measure of entrepreneurial responsiveness, subject to the extent of the cost-saving between size classes. On this basis all the regions except the South show a high degree of responsiveness. However, it is not clear whether the problem in the South was one of low entrepreneurial response to market signals or whether such market forces themselves were marginal.

B. Optimal Plant Sizes by Industry and Region, 1850-1870.

While the survivor technique results at the aggregate regional level are historically interesting, the survivor principle is strictly applicable only to well defined industry groups. In particular, the patterns at the aggregate regional level may reflect nothing more than differing industry mixes between the regions and over the years.

1. Intra-Regional Traded Goods.

Table 10.3 presents the survivor technique estimates for flour milling. The results show a wide variety of plant sizes surviving ranging from some of the very smallest to some of the largest. Most of the results have been labelled inconsistent because some intervening size groups underwent a decline in their share of value-added between 1850 and 1870. This may simply reflect random changes though a case could be made for arguing that the small, highly localized flour mill was destined to go out of business in the next decade or so as transportation increased competition particularly from the mills using the new process and as these mills established some form of brand identity and loyalty. The results also indicate that between 47 and 99 percent of the nation's flour was being produced in plants that were optimally sized and that even higher percentages were produced by plants that were minimally efficient in their scale of operation.

The survivor estimates for lumber milling are given in Table 10.4. Like those for flour milling, if the existence of random changes is denied, the results would seem to be inconsistent with a unimodal long-run average cost curve because of the simultaneous growth of two non-adjacent size groups. Even the very small saw mills appear to have been able to survive although their days, like those of the small local flour mill, were probably numbered because of the spread of the transportation system which opened local areas to competition from plants that enjoyed especially favorable locations.

Overall, optimally sized plants produced between 35 and 95 percent of all industry value-added depending upon the region. The shift in the industry for the New England states to the mid-western states is also apparent from the estimates. The minimum efficient plant in each region was larger than in the other regions and was largest in the mid-west where firms such as Weyerhauser were beginning to grow and expand.

2. Inter-Regionally Traded Commodities.

The survivor technique estimates for the three inter-regionally traded commodities are shown in Tables 10.5, 10.6 and 10.7. The results, particularly

Table 10.3

Optimal Size Categories of Plant and Minimum Efficient
Plant Size by Region 1850-1870 for Flour Milling

Region	Optimal Plant Size	Percentage of Total Value-Added Produced in Optimally Sized Plants 1850	Percentage of Total Value-Added Produced in Optimally Sized Plants 1870	Minimum Efficient Plant Size	Status
Middle Atlantic	D,F	22.4	74.9	D	Unclear and Inconsistent[1]
New England	A,D-F	43.3	94.0	A	Unclear and Inconsistent[1]
Pacific	A,G-I	38.5	61.6	A	Unclear and Inconsistent
South	G-J	17.3	48.4	H	Clear
West	A,C-F,H	71.4	98.9	A	Unclear and Inconsistent
United States	A-B,D,I	30.9	47.3	A	Unclear and Inconsistent[1]

[1] Inconsistency resolved by merging size categories.

Table 10.4

Optimal Size Categories of Plant and Minimum Efficient
Plant Size by Region 1850-1870 for Lumber Milling

Region	Optimal Plant Size	Percentage of Total Value-Added Produced in Optimally Sized Plants 1850	1870	Minimum Efficient Plant Size	Status
Middle Atlantic	C-E	34.2	89.2	C	Unclear
New England	D-J	67.7	95.2	D	Clear
Pacific	A-D, G-H	30.0	84.5	A	Unclear and Inconsistent
South	A, C-D, G	19.6	38.3	A	Unclear and Inconsistent[1]
West	F, H	14.7	35.6	F	Inconsistent[1]
United States	G, J	31.3	40.7	G	Unclear and Inconsistent

[1] Inconsistency resolved by merging size categories.

Table 10.5

Optimal Size Categories of Plant and Minimum Efficient
Plant Size by Region 1850-1870 for Boots and Shoes

Region	Optimal Plant Size(s)	Percentage of Total Value-Added Produced in Optimally Sized Plants 1850	1870	Minimum Efficient Plant Size	Status
Middle Atlantic	D,H	30.7	46.9	D	Unclear and Inconsistent
New England	G-I	37.5	49.1	G	Unclear
Pacific	A-E	15.7	100.0	A	Unclear
South	F-G	0.0	49.0	F	Clear
West	A-B,F,I	19.3	55.3	A	Inconsistent
United States	H-I	15.9	32.4	H	Unclear

Table 10.6

Optimal Size Categories of Plant and Minimum Efficient
Plant Size by Region 1850-1870 for Clothing

Region	Optimal Plant Size	Percentage of Total Value-Added Produced in Optimally Sized Plants 1850	1870	Minimum Efficient Plant Size	Status
Middle Atlantic	D-E	63.5	100.0	D	Clear
New England	B-F	41.1	100.0	B	Clear
Pacific	E-F	0.0	100.0	E	Clear
South	G-J	48.7	77.9	G	Clear
West	C-D	20.0	65.2	C	Clear
United States	G-J	36.8	67.3	G	Clear

Table 10.7

Optimal Size Categories of Plant and Minimum Efficient
Plant Size by Region 1850-1870 for Cotton Goods

Region	Optimal Plant Size	Percentage of Total Value-Added Produced in Optimally Sized Plants 1850	1870	Minimum Efficient Plant Size	Status
Middle Atlantic	J	0.0	88.5	J	Clear
New England	G-J	60.0	96.8	G	Clear
South	I	0.0	74.7	I	Clear
United States	I-J	14.6	90.4	I	Clear

these for clothing and for cotton goods in Tables 10.6 and 10.7 respectively, present fewer problems of interpretation than those for the locally traded commodities in so far as the majority of the results are coded as "clear". For these industries there existed a clear range of surviving plants.

The minimum efficient plant size in each of these factory industries is much larger than the minimum efficient plant in the local or handicraft industries as might be anticipated and the range of surviving plants also tends to be rather more restricted implying that for these industries the U-shape of the long-run average cost curve may be more pronounced. As for the intra-regionally traded commodities the percent of value-added produced in optimally sized plants is quite high. In each case though the percentage of value-added from optimally sized plants is lowest in the south. This is also true for the intra-regionally traded commodities. The extent of adjustment to optimality therefore seems to be least in the South and greatest in New England and the Middle Atlantic states. This may then be the source of any competitive failing by southern manufacturers for none is apparent on the basis of the production function estimates given above. It is not that the "typical" firm in the South was non-competitive (in the sense of producing under increasing or decreasing returns to scale and decreasing or increasing unit costs) but rather that too much of her industry vis a vis conditions in other regions fell outside the optimal range. At the same time, if one examines the relative change in value-added in optimally sized plants between 1850 and 1870 then the South appears in a more favorable light. The relative change in value-added produced in optimally sized plants was either greatest for the South or not very different from that in the New England states. This may be viewed as a measure of entrepreneurial responsiveness, in which case the entrepreneurs in the South appear to be as, or more, responsive than entrepreneurs elsewhere. Thus the relative low percentage of value-added in optimally-sized plants may just reflect that the South found itself in the 1840s with a backward industrial structure when compared with the other regions. Once recognized, the southern entrepreneur appears to have responded with as much vigor as his competitors in other regions.

Comparing the survivor technique estimates of the optimal or minimum efficient plant size with the variable scale elasticity estimates in Chapter 9 shows that the two techniques are consistent with each other. In each region the minimum efficient plant in those industries producing interregionally traded commodities was producing under conditions of constant returns to scale and this coincided with the range of optimally-sized plants. In the production of intra-regionally traded commodities the minimum efficient plant was typically producing under increasing returns to scale, but over some part of the range of optimally sized plants there existed constant returns to scale. This is consistent with the characteristics and nature of these local industries as we have discussed them above.

Where the largest of the optimally sized plants are operating under conditions of decreasing returns to scale on the basis of the variable scale elasticity production function estimates in Chapter 9, then it may be that there exist some external economies. This was most pronounced in those industries where such externalities are most likely to arise as in cotton textiles.

Finally, the results suggest that there existed a clear and pronounced trend towards concentration in large manufacturing establishments which predates the merger movement of the 1880s and 1890s. This trend is apparent in all regions and there is no evidence of markedly different entrepreneurial responses between the regions.

CHAPTER 11

CONCLUSION

The conclusions of this thesis are not particularly surprising, at least to economists, but they are of considerable importance to much of the current historical research and cast doubt upon the conclusions of earlier works. According to the estimates I present, constant returns to scale cannot be asserted as an iron law governing mid-nineteenth century industrial production, even though, in general, I could not reject the hypothesis that most industries operated under conditions of constant or decreasing returns to scale. The most notable exceptions to this characterization were the intra-regionally traded commodities (flour and lumber in this analysis) where the weight of evidence pointed instead towards increasing returns to scale. These industries were also the most typical of the mid-nineteenth century industrial structure in America. In the production of inter-regionally traded commodities, decreasing returns to scale were more the order of the day.

The evidence then in favor of the Russel-Linden-Genovese hypothesis is scant. Of the three assumptions implicit in it, only one is supported by the evidence and that is, that over some range of outputs there are scale economies to be realized. For the most part, however, manufacturers had already taken advantage of these and expanded into the range of approximately constant returns to scale. Large plant size was not a prerequisite for realizing scale economies. Moreover, there is no really convincing evidence that production conditions differed markedly between the southern states and the north-eastern states.

Evidence gleaned from the variable scale elasticity production function estimates suggests that, even though cross-sectional production conditions were remarkably similar over the regions, there may exist some external economies available only to large firms. These externalities seem to have been most pronounced in the Middle Atlantic and New England states and they may thus be related to the level and extent of manufacturing development. The external economies permitted large firms in those regions to have lower unit production costs than smaller firms even where those smaller firms were operating under conditions of constant returns to scale. However, large size was not a prerequisite to realize internal scale economies and operate under constant returns.

The conclusions regarding the large firms were supported by the results from the survivor technique. There would seem to have been a trend towards concentration in American industry that predates the merger movement of the 1880s and that this trend was based on external rather than internal scale economies.

In its overall conclusions regarding the extent of scale economies in the mid-nineteenth century, the results are very similar to those obtained for the twentieth century and reported by Walters, Besen, Ferguson, Moroney and others that the hypothesis of constant returns to scale cannot be rejected. The results therefore provide some empirical basis for the assumption of constant returns to scale made by Temin and Williamson.

However, Williamson's assumption though that labor received 55 percent of national income seems overly optimistic. The production function estimates imply a labor share of 40-50 percent of national income between 1850 and 1870 and the 1850 and 1860 estimates are very similar to those made by Budd using different methodology.

The estimates for the cotton industry also appear very similar to those made by David for a different data set. Indeed this consistency reinforces my confidence in the accuracy and validity of these production function estimates. Further supportive evidence is presented in the Appendix which gives the regional and national estimates for twelve two-digit S.I.C. industries.

Footnotes to Chapter 1

[1] See Temin (1966), Fogel (1967), Uselding (1970), Temin (1971) and David (1975).

[2] A production function is homogeneous of degree $\underline{k}$ if

$$f(tL, tK) = t^k f(L,K)$$

where $\underline{k}$ is as constant and $\underline{t}$ is any positive number. If both inputs are increased by the factor $\underline{t}$, output is increased by the factor $\underline{t}^k$. Returns to scale are decreasing if k<1, constant if k=1, and increasing if k>1.

[3] Temin (1966)

[4] Williamson (1974) and Williamson (1975)

[5] Douglas (1934)

[6] Walters (1963), 27

[7] Ibid., 34

[8] Brown and Popkin (1962)

[9] Bodkin and Klein (1967)

[10] Brown and Popkin (1962), 408 and 410

[11] Bodkin and Klein (1967), 42

[12] Hildebrand and Liu (1965). The Hildebrand and Liu results would show approximately constant returns to scale across industries if their surprisingly large estimate of the output elasticity with respect to technology is discarded. Inclusion of this variable is criticized by Griliches' (1966) review of Hildebrand and Liu.

[13] Griliches (1967) and Griliches (1968)

[14] Ibid., 156

[15] Besen (1967)

[16] Ferguson (1967)

[17] Moroney (1967)

[18] Ferguson (1967), 215

[19]The term "availability" is used loosely to the extent that all data, where not lost or destroyed, are available in the manuscript censuses of manufactures. This study used randomly selected firm data from the manuscript censuses of 1850, 1860, and 1870, collected by Professor Fred Bateman and Professor Thomas Weiss using funds provided by the National Science Foundation. Professor James Foust was also involved with the project and research assistance was provided by Jeremy Atack.

[20]Gray (1933), 529-544

[21]Dickey and Wilson (1972) unpublished paper

[22]Gray's approach is not a true survivor technique since he looks at increases in the relative concentration of slaveholdings.

[23]Economies of scale are a purely production phenomenon and are identified by the degree of homogeneity of the production function given by the sum of the output elasticities of the firm's inputs. A priori, there can be no presumption of a relationship between firm size and economies of scale. In general, however, as the results in Chapter 9 indicate large firms are generally producing in the area of constant or decreasing returns to scale, that is, they have achieved all of the potential economies of scale in production. The difference is subtle but important. Small firms as shown in Chapter 9 produce under conditions of increasing returns to scale, i.e., economies of scale, which larger firms have already achieved. More importantly, current usage of the term "economies of scale" confuses returns to scale and economies of size. See, for example, Maxwell (1970).

[24]Fogel and Engerman (1974)

[25]Ibid., volume II, 143

[26]Ibid., 126-142

[27]Walsh (1972)

[28]Ibid., 142

[29]Ibid., 159

[30]Ibid., 200

[31]David (1970) and David (1975)

[32]David (1975), 142

[33]Ibid., 143

[34]Russel (1938), 47

[35] Linden (1940). Linden makes an error in quoting the article by Taylor in De Bow's Review (1850) which gives the salary range as $1,200 to $1,500.

[36] Genovese (1961) and Genovese (1962)

[37] Genovese (1962), 430

[38] Eighth Census (1865)

[39] De Bow's Review (1850), 509

[40] Fogel and Engerman (1974), volume I, 249

Footnotes to Chapter 2

[1] The distinction between the ex ante and ex post production function was first made by Johansen (1959). See also Johansen (1972).

[2] McFadden (1963), Mundlak (1968 and Solow (1967)

[3] Kmenta and Joseph (1963)

[4] Hoch (1963)

[5] Marschak and Andrews (1944)

[6] Zellner, Kmenta and Dreze (1966)

[7] Under conditions of imperfect competition, disturbances to the production function will be transmitted to the factor and output markets. To the extent that the disturbances are transmitted there is at least one missing equation in the model. See Mundlak and Hoch (1965).

[8] See Zellner, Kmenta and Dreze (1966). A necessary condition for the identification of the production function is that relative prices vary exogenously. See Bridge (1971). However, the restrictions imposed upon the variance-covariance matrix in the Zellner et al. model are sufficient to ensure identification.

[9] Maddala and Kadane (1967)

[10] Bodkin and Klein (1967)

[11] Kmenta and Joseph (1963)

[12] Ibid., 384-385

[13] The advantages of this firm were first suggested by Griliches (1967) and developed in Griliches (1968) and Griliches and Ringstad (1971).

[14] Maddala and Kadana (1967)

[15] Kmenta (1967). However, this formulation was circulated by him for a number of years prior to its formal publication.

[16] Maddala and Kadana (1967). See also Table 2.1.

[17] See, for example, Lu and Fletcher (1968), Sato and Hoffman (1968) and Clemhout (1968).

[18] For example, assuming $\mu=1$ (constant returns to scale):

The Coefficient of the Squared
Capital-Labor Ratio for
Various Assumed Values of ρ and δ.

ρ	δ .1	.2	.3	.4	.5	Implied σ
5	-.225	-.40	-.525	-.60	-.625	0.17
2	-.09	-.16	-.21	-.24	-.25	0.33
1	-.045	-.08	-.105	-.12	-.125	0.50
-.1	.005	.008	.011	.012	.013	1.11
-.5	.023	.040	.053	.060	.063	2
-.9	.041	.072	.095	.108	.113	10

[19] Kmenta (1967)

[20] A production function is said to be homothetic if the elasticity of substitution between two inputs depends only upon the ratio of those inputs, that is, if the elasticity of substitution is independent of scale. If a production function is homothetic, then the isoquants are radial projections of one another so that the slope of the isoquants at any point along a ray from the origin is constant. If a production function is homogeneous then it is also homothetic, however, not all homothetic production functions are necessarily homogeneous.

[21] See Nerlove (1963), Soskice (1968), Zellner and Revankar (1969), and Ringstad (1974).

[22] Ringstad (1974), 89

[23] Griliches and Ringstad (1971), 10

[24] Nerlove (1963) and Ringstad (1974)

[25] Zellner and Revankar (1969)

[26] Ringstad (1974)

[27] Friedman (1955)

[28] There is an ever present tendency to equate economies of scale and economies of size. Economies of scale are defined strictly in terms of the homogeneity of the production function, while economies of size are shown by the shape of the long-run average cost function. Maintaining the distinction between these two concepts permits resolution of the dichotomy in which a firm subject to constant returns to scale has indeterminate optimal plant size. Plant size under this distinction becomes determinate due to economies of size which permit the purchase of inputs for a lower unit cost. Unfortunately, the use of dollar values as proxies for the physical quantities in the estimation of production functions clouds this distinction. See Maxwell (1970).

[29] Johnston (1960) and Walters (1963)

[30] Friedman (1955)

[31] Stigler (1958) and Stigler (1950)

[32] See Saving (1961), Weiss (1964), Weiss (1965a), Weiss (1965b). Practical use of this technique has been made by Bain (1956), Pratten and Dean (1965), and Scherer (1974).

[33] Shepherd (1967)

[34] Ibid.

[35] Ibid., especially 114-116

[36] Ibid., 116

Footnotes to Chapter 3

[1] Work on this project was funded by the National Science Foundation under Grant GS-2450. The project was conducted by Professor Fred Bateman of Indiana University and Professor Thomas Weiss of the University of Kansas. Professor James D. Foust was involved with the early stages of data collection.

[2] See Wright (1900).

[3] All information contained in the censuses is available from the Bateman-Weiss worksheets from the selected firms. Furthermore only two items of information have not been coded on punch cards—the name of the establishment and the page and line references from the census manuscripts.

[4] The neglected items are: name of the establishment, type of raw materials and type of output, the number of motive power units and the county in which the establishment was located.

[5] See, for example, Niemi (1974) but others such as Walsh (1969) are more careful.

[6] Creamer (1960). For a further discussion of the problem, see Bateman, Foust and Weiss (1975).

[7] Fourteenth Census (1923).

[8] Twelfth Census (1902).

[9] Eleventh Census (1895).

[10] Fogel (1964).

[11] Eleventh Census (1895).

[12] This is discussed more fully by Bateman, Foust and Weiss (1975).

[13] Griliches (1967) and Griliches and Ringstad (1971).

[14] That is, chapter 8 below.

[15] Eleventh Census (1895). See also Bateman, Foust and Weiss (1975).

[16] See Maxwell (1970).

Footnotes to Chapter 4

[1] Maddala and Kadane (1967)

[2] Galbraith (1952)

[3] See David (1970)

[4] David (1970) and (1975)

Footnotes to Chapter 5

[1] See, for example, Bateman and Weiss (1974) and Bateman and Weiss (1975b).

[2] U.S. Bureau of the Census (1967)

[3] Ibid.

[4] Bateman and Weiss (1975b)

[5] See Seventh Census (1859), Eighth Census (1865) and Ninth Census (1872).

[6] Bateman and Weiss (1975b) and Bateman and Weiss (1976)

[7] Bateman and Weiss (1975b), 316-317

[8] Genovese (1961)

[9] Bateman and Weiss (1975b)

[10] Schmidt (1920)

[11] Kuhlmann (1929)

[12] Ibid.

[13] Ibid.

[14] Swisher (1940), and Kuhlmann (1929)

[15] Eleventh Census (1896)

[16] Bateman and Weiss (1976)

[17] The circular rip saw was introduced from England about 1814 and was widely adopted after 1830. See Compton (1916), Larson (1949), and Reynolds (1957).

Footnotes to Chapter 6

[1] Keir (1920)

[2] Manuscript census data. This estimate is also supported by Keir (1920), 228.

[3] Hazard (1921)

[4] *Ibid.*

[5] Manuscript census data

[6] Keir (1920)

[7] Genovese (1960) and (1961)

[8] Smith (1850)

[9] *Ibid.*

[10] Hammond (1850)

[11] Keir (1920)

[12] Bishop (1868), II, 509

[13] *Ibid.*, 492

[14] *Ibid.*, 507

[15] *Ibid.*, III, 435

[16] Zevin (1971) and (1975)

[17] See Appendix, especially Tables A.3, A.15 and A.27.

[18] Zevin (1975)

[19] David (1971) and (1975)

[20] McGouldrick (1968)

[21] David (1975)

[22] De Bow (1850)

Footnotes to Chapter 7

[1] Budd (1960)

[2] See chapter 1, especially notes 34-36

[3] Manuscript census data

[4] Budd (1960)

[5] *Ibid*.

Footnotes to Chapter 8

[1] For the Cobb-Douglas production function, the marginal products of labor and capital are defined as:

$$\frac{\partial V}{\partial L} = \alpha \cdot \frac{V}{L} = MP_L; \quad \frac{\partial V}{\partial K} = \beta \cdot \frac{V}{K} = MP_K$$

Therefore, changing the measure of K(or L) with V constant leads to a compensating change in the magnitude of β(or α).

[2] Buildings were assumed to have a lifespan of fifty years and machinery, a lifespan of fifteen years. Zero Scrap value was assumed and the ratios of investment in buildings and machinery to capital investment were derived from the Eleventh Census as described in Chapter 3.

[3] Using the ratio of insurance, maintenance and repair expenditures to capital investment from the Eleventh Census. See Chapter 3.

[4] Twenty-nine percent was chosen as the opportunity cost measures based upon Bateman and Weiss' estimates of the mean profit rate in 1860. See Fred Bateman and Thomas Weiss (1975a)

[5] Based on the Eleventh Census data on the ratio of "live assets" to output. See Chapter 3.

[6] Maddala and Kadane (1967)

[7] This is not considered by David (1970 and 1975) who confines his attention to the Cobb-Douglas form.

Footnotes to Chapter 9

[1] Nerlove (1963) and Nerlove (1965)

[2] Ringstad (1974)

[3] Zellner and Revankar (1969)

[4] Ringstad (1974)

[5] Box and Cox (1963)

[6] For the Nerlove transformation:

$$\prod_{i=1}^{n} (1 + 2\phi \log V_i) = \sum_{i=1}^{n} \log(1 + 2\phi \log V_i)$$

and for the Ringstad:

$$\prod_{i=1}^{n} (1 + 2\phi \log V_i + \Theta V_i) = \sum_{i=1}^{n} \log(1 + 2\phi \log V_i + \Theta V_i)$$

[7] Zellner and Revankar (1969)

[8] *Ibid.*

[9] Ringstad (1974)

[10] Atack (1977)

[11] Atack and Bateman (1977)

[12] Atack (1977)

[13] *Ibid.*

Footnotes to Chapter 10

[1] See Stigler (1958), Saving (1961), Weiss (1964) and Shepherd (1967).

[2] Shepherd (1967)

[3] Stigler (1958)

[4] See, for example, Walters (1963)

[5] Shepherd (1967)

[6] Ibid.

[7] Friedman (1955)

[8] Shepherd (1967)

[9] Weiss (1964)

[10] See, for example, Stigler (1958) and Saving (1961)

[11] Production function estimates are also biased and may be inconsistent when applied to monopolistic industries. See, for example, Nerlove (1965).

[12] That is, small plants operate under conditions of increasing returns to scale while larger plants under constant returns eventually giving way to decreasing returns to scale for the very largest plant.

[13] Assuming perfect competition (factor input prices constant and increases in production by the firm do not affect market price) then if the returns to scale parameter is .75, a doubling of inputs will increase output by a factor of 1.75 and hence raise unit costs by a factor of 2/1.75 = 1.143.

[14] Ware (1931)

[15] Keir (1920)

BIBLIOGRAPHY

Aigner, D. J., and Chu, S. F. (1968), "On Estimating the Industry Production Function," American Economic Review, Vol. 58, pp. 826-839.

Aitken, A. C. (1934-1935), "On Least Squares and Linear Combinations of Observations," Proceedings of the Royal Statistical Society, Edinburgh, Vol. 55, pp. 42-48.

Aitken, A. C. (1948), "On the Estimation of Many Statistical Parameters," Proceedings of the Royal Statistical Society, Edinburgh, Vol. 62, pp. 369-377.

Aldrich Report (1892), Retail Prices and Wages, Washington, D.C., Senate Committee on Finances, Report 986.

Aldrich, Mark (1973), "Flexible Exchange Rates, Northern Expansion, and the Market for Southern Cotton," Journal of Economic History, Vol. 33, pp. 399-416.

Andreano, Ralph, editor (1972), The Impact of the American Civil War, Second Edition, Cambridge, Massachusetts: Schenkman.

Arrow, Kenneth; Hurwicz, L.; and Uzana, H. (1958), "Studies in Linear and Non-Linear Programming," Stanford Mathematical Studies in the Social Sciences, II, Stanford: Stanford University Press.

Arrow, Kenneth; Karlin, Samuel; and Suppes, Patrick, editors (1960), Mathematical Methods in the Social Sciences, Stanford: Stanford University Press.

Arrow, Kenneth; Chenery, H. B.; Minhas and Solow, R. M. (1961), "Capital-Labor Substitution and Economic Effiency," Review of Economics and Statistics, Vol. 43, pp. 225-250.

Atack, Jeremy (1977), "Returns to Scale in Antebellum United States Manufacturing," Explorations in Economic History, 14, pp. 337-359.

Atack, Jeremy and Bateman, Fred (1977), "The Survivor Technique and Identification of Optimal Plant Size Using Individual Plant Data," University of Illinois unpublished paper (xerox).

Bain, Joe S. (1956), Barriers to New Competition, Cambridge, Massachusetts: Harvard University Press.

Barankin, E. and Dorfman, R. (1958), "On Quadratic Programming," Berkeley Series in Statistics, Berkeley: University of California Press.

Barrett, Nancy Smith (1974), *The Theory of Microeconomic Policy*, Lexington, Massachusetts: D. C. Heath.

Bateman, Fred; Foust, James D.; and Weiss, Thomas J. (1971), "Large Scale Manufacturing in the South and West, 1850-1860," *Business History Review*, Vol. 45, pp. 1-17.

Bateman, Fred; Foust, James D.; and Weiss, Thomas J. (1974), "The Participation of Planters in Manufacturing in the Antebellum South," *Agricultural History*, Vol. 48, pp. 277-298.

Bateman, Fred and Weiss, Thomas J. (September, 1974), "Comparative Regional Development in Antebellum Manufacturing," paper presented to the Economic History Association, (mimeo).

Bateman, Fred and Weiss, Thomas J. (November, 1974), "Profitability and Industrialization in the Antebellum Southern Economcy," paper presented to the Southern Historical Association, (mimeo).

Bateman, Fred; Foust, James D.; and Weiss, Thomas J. (1975a), "Profitability in Southern Manufacturing: Estimates for 1860," *Explorations in Economic History*, Vol. 12, pp. 211-231.

Bateman, Fred and Weiss, Thomas J. (1975b), "Market Structures Before the Age of Big Business: Concentration and Profit in Early Southern Manufacturing," *Business History Review*.

Bateman, Fred and Weiss, Thomas J. (1976), "Manufacturing in the Antebellum South," in P. Uselding ed., *Research in Economic History*, 1, Greenwich, Conn.: Jai Press.

Beale, E. M. L. (1955), "On Minimizing a Convex Function Subject to Linear Inequalities," *Journal of the Royal Statistical Society*, Series B, Vol. 17, pp. 173-184.

Beard, Charles A. and Beard, Mary R. (1930), *The Rise of American Civilization*, New York: Macmillian.

Besen, Stanley M. (1967), "Elasticities of Substitution and Returns to Scale in United States Manufacturing: Some Additional Evidence," *Southern Economic Journal*, Vol. 34, pp. 280-282.

Bishop, Leander J. (1868), *A History of American Manufacturers from 1608-1860*, Philadelphia: Edward Young and Co., 3 volumes.

Bodkin, Ronald G. and Klein, Lawrence R. (1967), "Nonlinear Estimation of Aggregate Production Functions," *The Review of Economics and Statistics*, Vol. 49, pp. 28-44.

Bogue, Allan G. (1963), *From Prairies to Corn Belt: Farming on the Illinois and Iowa Prairies in the Nineteenth Century*, Chicago: University of Chicago Press.

Boot, J. C. B. (1963), "Constraint Procedures of Quadratic Programming," *Econometrica*, Vol. 31, pp. 464-498.

Borts, G. H. and Mishan, E. J. (1962), "Exploring the 'Uneconomic Region' of the Production Function," *Review of Economic Studies*, Vol. 9, pp. 300-312.

Box, G. E. P. and Cox, D. R. (1963), "An Analysis of Transformations," *Journal of the Royal Statistical Society*, Series B, Vol. 26, pp. 211-252.

Brady, Dorothy S. (1966), "Price Deflators for Final Product Estimates," *Output, Employment and Productivity in the United States After 1800*, NBER, Studies in Income and Wealth, Vol. 30, Princeton: Princeton University Press, pp. 91-116.

Bridge, J. L. (1971), *Applied Econometrics*, Amsterdam: North-Holland.

Bronfenbrenner, M. (1944), "Production Functions: Cobb-Douglas, Inter-Firm, Intra-Firm," *Econometrica*, Vol. 12, pp. 33-34.

Brown, Murray and Popkins, Joel (1962), "A Measure of Technological Change and Returns to Scale," *The Review of Economics and Statistics*, Vol. 44, pp. 402-411.

Budd, Edward C. (1960), "Factor Shares, 1850-1910," in *Trends in the American Economy in the Nineteenth Century*, NBER, Studies in Income and Wealth, 24, Princeton: Princeton University Press.

Burns, Arthur and Mitchell, Wesley (1946), *Measuring Business Cycles*, New York: NBER.

Carlson, Sune (1956), *A Study on the Pure Theory of Production*, New York: Kelley and Millman.

Carter, Hodding (1959), *The Angry Scar: The Story of Reconstruction 1865-1877*, New York: Doubleday and Sons.

Charnes, A; Cooper, W. W.; and Ferguson (1955), "Optimal Estimation of Executive Compensation by Linear Programming," *Management Science*, Vol. 1, pp. 138-151.

Chipman, J. S. and Rao, M. M. (1964), "The Treatment of Linear Restrictions in Regression Analysis," *Econometrica*, Vol. 32, pp. 198-209.

Christ, C. F., editor (1963), *Measurement in Economics*, Stanford: Stanford University Press.

Chu, S. F.; Aigner, D. J.; and Frankel, M. (1970), "On the Log-Quadratic Law of Production," *Southern Economic Journal*, Vol. 37, pp. 32-39.

Clemhout, S. (1968), "The Class of Homothetic Isoquant Production Functions," *Review of Economic Studies*, Vol. 35, pp. 91-104.

Cochran, Thomas C. (1951), "Business Organization and the Development of an Industrial Discipline," Harold F. Williamson, editor, *The Growth of the American Economy*, Second Edition, Englewood Cliffs: Prentice-Hall, Inc., pp. 279-295.

Cochran, Thomas C. (1961), "Did the Civil War Retard Industrialization," *Mississippi Valley Historical Review*, Vol. 48, pp. 191-210.

Coelho, P. R. P. and Shepherd, J. F. (1974), "Differences in Regional Prices: The United States, 1851-1880," *Journal of Economic History*, Vol. 34, pp. 551-591.

Conrad, Alfred H. and Meyer, John R. (1968), "The Economics of Slavery in the Antebellum South," *Journal of Political Economy*, Vol. 66, pp. 95-122.

Cobb, C. W. (1930), "Production in Massachusetts Manufacturing, 1890-1928," *Journal of Political Economy*, Vol. 38, pp. 705-707.

Cobb, C. W. and Douglas, P. H. (1928), "A Theory of Production," *American Economic Review*, Vol. 18 (Supplement), pp. 139-165.

Coulter, Merton E. (1947), *The South During Reconstruction, 1865-1877*, Baton Rouge: Louisiana State University Press, 1947.

Creamer, D. (1960), *Capital in Manufacturing and Mining*, Princeton: Princeton University Press.

Crockett, Norman L. (1969), "The Westward Movement and the Transit of American Machine Technology: The Case of Wool Manufacturing," *Nebraska Journal of Economics and Business*, Vol. 8, pp. 111-120.

Crockett, Norman L. (1970), *The Woolen Industry of the Mid-West*, Lexington, Kentucky: University Press of Kentucky.

Crompton, William (1916), *The Organization of the Lumber Industry*, Chicago: American Lumberman.

David, Paul A. (1970), "Learning by Doing and Tariff Protection: A Reconsideration of the Case of Ante-Bellum United States Cotton Textile Industry," *Journal of Economic History*, Vol. 30, pp. 521-601.

David, Paul A. (1975), *Technical Choice, Innovation and Economic Growth*, London: Cambridge University Press.

Dantzig, G. B. (1961), "Quadratic Programming: A Variant of the Wolfe-Markowitz Algorithm," *Operations Reseach Center*, Berkeley: University of California.

Davis, Lance E. (1958), "Sources of Industrial Finance: The American Textile Industry, A Case Study," *Explorations in Entrepreneurial History*, Vol. 9, pp. 190-203.

Davis, Lance E. (1960), "The New England Textile Mills and the Capital Markets: A Study of Industrial Borrowing, 1840-1860," *Journal of Economic History*, Vol. 20, pp. 1-20.

Davis, Lance and Stettler, H. Louis (1966), "The New England Textile Industry 1825-1860: Fluctuations and Trends," *Output, Employment and Productivity in the United States after 1800*, New York: NBER, pp. 213-238.

Davis, Lance E. (1971), "Capital Mobility and American Growth," Robert W. Fogel and Stanley L. Engerman, editors, *The Reinterpretation of American Economic History*, New York: Harper and Row, pp. 285-300.

Davis, Lance; Easterlin, Richard A.; Parker, William N., *et al*. (1972), *American Economic Growth*, New York: Harper and Row.

De Bow, J. D. B. (published monthly from January 1846-June 1880 with omissions), *De Bow's Review: Agricultural, Commercial Industrial Progress and Resources*, New Orleans.

Dickey, G. Edward and Wilson, Warren W. (1972), "Economies of Scale in Cotton Agriculture, 1850-1860," unpublished paper, (mineo).

Diwan, R. K. (November 1966), "Alternative Specifications of Economies of Scale," *Econometrica*, Vol. 33, pp. 442-452.

Diwan, R. K. (1968), "On the Cobb-Douglas Production Function," *Southern Economic Journal*, Vol. 34, pp. 410-414.

Douglas, Paul H. (1934), *The Theory of Wages*, New York.

Drummond, Ian M. (1967), "Labor Scarcity and the Problem of American Industrial Efficiency in the 1850's: A Comment," *Journal of Economic History*, Vol. 27, pp. 383-390.

Easterlin, Richard A. (1960), "Inter-Regional Differences in Per Capita Income, Population, and Total Income, 1840-1950," *Trends in the American Economy in the Nineteenth Century*, NBER, Princeton: Princeton University Press.

Easterlin, Richard A. (1961), "Regional Income Trends, 1840-1950," Seymour E. Harris, editor, *American Economic History*, New York: McGraw-Hill, pp. 525-547.

Eighth Census (1865), *Manufacturers of the United States in 1860*, Washington, D.C.: Government Printing Office.

Eleventh Census (1895), *Report on Manufacturing Industries in the United States at the Eleventh Census*, Washington, D.C.: Government Printing Office.

Engerman, Stanley L. (1966), "The Economic Impact of the Civil War," *Explorations in Entrepreneurial History*, Series 2, Vol. 3, pp. 176-199.

Farrell, M. J. (1957), "The Measurement of Productive Efficiency," *Journal of the Royal Statistical Society*, Series A, Vol. 120, pp. 253-281.

Farrell, M. J. and Fieldhouse, M. (1963), "Estimating Efficient Production Under Increasing Returns to Scale," *Journal of the Royal Statistical Society*, Series A, Vol. 125, pp. 252-257.

Fenichel, Allan H. (1966), "Growth and Diffusion of Power in Manufacturing, 1838-1919," *Output, Employment and Productivity in the United States after 1800*, Studies in Income and Wealth, Vol. 30, NBER, pp. 3-76.

Ferguson, C. E. (1965), "Substitution, Technical Progress and Returns to Scale," *American Economic Review* (Proceedings), Vol. 55, pp. 296-305.

Ferguson, C. E. (1967), "Substitution, Relative Shares, and Returns to Scale: Some Statistical Regularities and Curiosa," *Southern Economic Journal*, Vol. 34, pp. 209-222.

Ferguson, C. E. (1972), *Microeconomic Theory*, Homewood: Richard D. Irwin, Inc. (Third Edition).

Fisher, Franklin M. (1969), "Existence of Aggregate Production Functions," *Econometrica*, Vol. 37, pp. 533-577.

Fleming, Walter L. (1919), *The Sequel to Appomattox*, New Haven: Yale University Press.

Fogel, Robert W. (1964), *Railroads and American Economic Growth*, Baltimore: Johns Hopkins University Press.

Fogel, Robert W. (1967), "The Specification Problem in Economic History," *Journal of Economic History*, Vol. 27, pp. 283-308.

Fogel, Robert W. and Engerman, Stanley L. (1969), "A Model for the Explanation of Industrial Expansion During the Nineteenth Century: With an Application to the American Iron Industry," Journal of Political Economy, Vol. 77, pp. 306-328.

Fogel, Robert W. and Engerman, Stanley L. (1971), The Reinterpretation of American Economic History, New York: Harper and Row.

Fogel, Robert W. and Engerman, Stanley L. (1971), "The Economics of Slavery," Fogel and Engerman, editors, The Reinterpretation of American Economic History, New York: Harper and Row, pp. 311-341.

Fogel, Robert W. and Engerman, Stanley L. (1971), "The Relative Efficiency of Slavery: A Comparison of Northern and Southern Agriculture in 1860," Explorations in Economic History, Vol. 8, pp. 354-367.

Fogel, Robert W. and Engerman, Stanley L. (1974), Time on the Cross, Boston: Little, Brown and Company, two volumes.

Fourteenth Census (1923), Manufacturers, 1919, Washington, D.C.: Government Printing Office.

Friedman, Milton (1955), "Comment," George J. Stigler, editor, Business Concentration and Price Policy, NBER, Princeton: Princeton University Press, pp. 230-238.

Friedman, Milton (1962), Price Theory, Chicago: Aldine Publishing Company.

Gallman, Robert E. (1960), "Commodity Output, 1839-1899," Trends in the American Economy in the Nineteenth Century, NBER, Studies in Income and Wealth, Vol. 24, Princeton: Princeton University Press, pp. 13-71.

Gallman, Robert E. and Weiss, Thomas J. (1969), "The Service Industries in the Nineteenth Century," V. R. Fuchs, editor, Production and Productivity in the Service Industries, NBER, Studies in Income and Wealth, Vol. 34, pp. 287-352.

Genovese, Eugene D. (1961), The Political Economy of Slavery, New York: Pantheon Books.

Genovese, Eugene D. (1962), "The Significance of the Slave Plantation for Southern Economic Development," Journal of Southern History, Vol. 28, pp. 422-437.

Gershenkron, A. (1962), Economic Backwardness in Historical Perspective, New York and London: Frederick A. Praeger.

Goldberger, Arthur S. (1968), "The Interpretation and Estimation of Cobb-Douglas Functions," Econometrica, Vol. 36, pp. 464-472.

Gray, Lewis Cecil (1933), History of Agriculture in the Southern United States to 1860, Washington, D.C.: Carnegie Institution, two volumes.

Gregg, William (1855), "Practical Results of Southern Manufactures," De Bow's Review, Vol. 18, pp. 777-791.

Griliches, Zvi (1966), "Book Review of 'Manufacturing Production Functions in the U.S., 1957,' by Hildebrand and Liu," Journal of Political Economy, Vol. 74, pp. 100-101.

Griliches, Zvi (1967), "Production Functions in Manufacturing: Some Preliminary Results," Murray Brown, editor, The Theory and Empirical Analysis of Production, NBER, Studies in Income and Wealth, Vol. 31, pp. 275-340.

Griliches, Zvi (1968), "Production Functions in Manufacturing: Some Additional Results," Southern Economic Journal, Vol. 35, pp. 151-156.

Griliches, Zvi and Ringstad, V. (1971), Economies of Scale and the Form of the Production Function, Amsterdam: North-Holland.

Habakkuk, H. J. (1962), American and British Technology in the Nineteenth Century, Cambridge, England: Cambridge University Press.

Hacker, Louis M. (1940), The Triumph of American Capitalism, New York: Columbia University Press.

Hammond, James H. (1850), "Address of Governor Hammond Before the South Carolina Institute," De Bow's Review, 8, p. 509.

Harris, Seymour E., editor (1961), American Economic History, New York: McGraw-Hill.

Hazard, Blanche E. (1913), "The Organization of the Boot and Shoe Industry Before 1875," Quarterly Journal of Economics, Vol. 27, pp. 236-262.

Henderson, J. M. and Quandt, R. E. (1971), Microeconomic Theory, New York: McGraw-Hill.

Hildebrand, G. M. and Liu, T. C. (1965), Manufacturing Production Functions in the U.S., 1957, Ithaca: Cornell University Press, Cornell Studies Number 15.

Hoch, I. (1958), "Simultaneous Equation Bias in the Context of the Cobb-Douglas Production Function," *Econometrica*, Vol. 26, pp. 34-53.

Hoch, I. (1962), "Estimation of Production Function Parameters Combining Time-Series and Cross Section Data," *Econometrica*, Vol. 30, pp. 556-578.

Hoch, Irving (1963), "Reply (to Kmenta and Joseph)," *Econometrica*, Vol. 31, pp. 386-388.

Hoover, Ethel (1958), "Wholesale and Retail Prices in the Nineteenth Century," *Journal of Economic History*, Vol. 28, pp. 298-316.

Hoover, Ethel (1960), "Retail Prices After 1850," *Trends in the American Economy in the Nineteenth Century*, NBER, Studies in Income and Wealth, Vol. 24, Princeton: Princeton University Press, pp. 141-190.

Houthakker, H. S. (1960), "The Capacity Method of Quadratic Programming," *Econometrica*, Vol. 28, pp. 62-87.

Hunt, F. (1839-1870), *Merchant's Magazine and Commercial Review*, New York. Otherwise known as *Hunt's Commercial Magazine*.

Hunter, Louis C. (1929), "The Influence of the Market upon Technique in the Iron Industry in Western Pennsylvania upto 1860," *Journal of Economics and Business History*, Vol. 1, pp. 241-281.

Johansen, L. (1959), "Substitution versus Fixed Production Coefficients in the Theory of Economic Growth: A Synthesis," *Econometrica*, Vol. 27, pp. 157-176.

Johansen, L. (1972), *Production Functions: An Integration of Micro and Macro, Short Run and Long Run Aspects*, Amsterdam: North-Holland.

Johnston, J. (1960), *Statistical Cost Functions*, New York: McGraw-Hill.

Johnston, J. (1972), *Econometric Methods*, New York: McGraw-Hill, Second Edition.

Judge, G. G. and Takayama, T. (1966), "Inequality Restrictions in Regression Analysis," *Journal of the American Statistical Association*, Vol. 61, pp. 49-61.

Kadiyala, Koteswara Rao (1970), "An Exact Small Sample Property of the k-Class Estimators," *Econometrica*, Vol. 38, pp. 930-932.

Karst, O. J. (1958), "Linear Curve Fitting Using Least Deviations," Journal of the American Statistical Association, Vol. 53, pp. 118–132.

Keir, Malcolm (1920), Manufacturing Industries in America, New York: The Ronald Press.

Kmenta, J. and Joseph, M. G. (1963), "A Monte Carlo Study of Alternative Estimates of the Cobb-Douglas Production Function," Econometrica, Vol. 31, pp. 363–385.

Kmenta, J. (1964), "Some Properties of Alternative Estimates of the Cobb-Douglas Production Function," Econometrica, Vol. 32, pp. 183–188.

Kmenta, J. (1967), "On Estimation of the CES Production Function," International Economic Review, Vol. 8, pp. 180–189.

Knowlton, Evelyn H. (1948), Pepperell's Progress: A History of a Cotton Textile Company, 1844–1945, Cambridge, Massachusetts: Harvard University Press.

Kuhlmann, Charles B. (1929), The Development of the Flour-Milling Industry in the United States, Boston: Houghton-Mifflin Co.

Kuhn, H. W. and Tucker, A. W. (1951), "Non-Linear Programming," J. Neyman, editor, Proceedings of the Second Berkeley Symposium on Mathematical Statistics and Probability, Berkeley: University of California Press, pp. 481–492.

Lander, Ernest M., Jr. (1969), The Textile Industry of Antebellum South Carolina, Baton Rouge: Louisiana State University Press.

Landes, David (1969), The Unbounded Prometheus, Cambridge, England: Cambridge University Press.

Larson, Agnes M. (1949), History of the White Pine Industry in Minnesota, Minneapolis: University of Minnesota Press.

Lebergott, Stanley (1966), "Labor Force and Employment, 1800–1960," Output, Employment and Productivity in the United States After 1800, Dorothy Brady, editor, NBER, Vol. 30.

Lebergott, Stanley (1964), Manpower in Economic Growth: The American Record Since 1800, New York: McGraw-Hill.

Lee, Everett S. (1957), Population Redistribution and Economic Growth, Philadelphia: American Philosophical Society.

Lee, T. C.; Judge, G. G.; and Zellner, A. (1970), Estimating the Parameters of the Markov Probability Model from Aggregate Time Series Data, Amsterdam: North-Holland.

Lerner, Eugene M. (1959), "Southern Output and Agricultural Income, 1860-1880," Agricultural History, Vol. 33, pp. 117-126.

Linden, Fabian (1940), "Repercussions of Manufacturing in the Antebellum South," North Carolina Historical Review, Vol. 17, pp. 313-331.

Lu, Y. and Fletcher, L. B. (1968), "A Generalization of the CES Production Function," Review of Economics and Statistics, Vol. 50, pp. 449-452.

Luenberger, D. G. (1973), Introduction to Linear and Non-Linear Programming, Reading, Massachusetts: Addison-Wesley.

Maddala, G. S. and Kadane, J. B. (1967), "Estimation of Returns to Scale and the Elasticity of Substitution," Econometrica, Vol. 35, pp. 419-423.

Malinvaud, E. (1970), Statistical Methods of Econometrics, Amsterdam: North-Holland, Revised Second Edition.

Marschak, J. and Andrews, W. J. (1944), "Random Simultaneous Equations and the Theory of Production," Econometrica, Vol. 12, pp. 143-205.

Maxwell, W. David (1970), Price Theory and It's Application in Business Administration, Pacific Palisades: Goodyear Publishing Company.

McFadden, D. (1963), "Further Results on CES Production Functions," Review of Economic Studies, Vol. 30, pp. 73-83.

McGouldrick, Paul F. (1968), New England Textile Mills in the Nineteenth Century: Profits and Investment, Cambridge, Mass.: Harvard University Press.

Means, Gardiner (1965), Economic Concentration, testimony to the Sub-Committee on Antitrust and Monopoly of the Committee of the Judiciary, U.S. Senate, 89th Congress, 1st Session Pt. 2, March-April, Washington, D.C.: Government Printing Office.

Meyer, Paul A. (1970), "An Aggregate Homothetic Production Function," Southern Economic Journal, Vol. 36, pp. 229-238.

Moroney, John R. (1967), "Cobb-Douglas Production Functions and Returns to Scale in U.S. Manufacturing Industry," Western Economic Journal, Vol. 6, pp. 39-51.

Moroney, John R. (1970), "Identification and Specification Analysis of Alternative Equations for Estimating the Elasticity of Substitution," Southern Economic Journal, Vol. 36, pp. 285-299.

Mundlak, Y. and Hoch, I. (1965), "Consequences of Alternative Specifications in Estimation of Cobb-Douglas Production Functions," Econometrica, Vol. 33, pp. 814-828.

Mundlak, Y. (1968), "Elasticities of Substitution and the Theory of Derived Demand," Review of Economic Studies, Vol. 35, pp. 225-236.

Nerlove, Marc (1963), "Returns to Scale in Electricity Supply," C. F. Christ, editor, Measurement in Economics, Stanford: Stanford University Press, pp. 167-198.

Nerlove, Marc (1965), The Estimation and Identification of Cobb-Douglas Production Functions, Amsterdam: North-Holland.

Niemi, Albert W. (1974), State and Regional Patterns in American Manufacturing 1860-1900, Westport, Connecticut: Greenwood Press.

Ninth Census (1872), Statistics of Wealth and Industry of the United States at the Ninth Census, Washington, D.C.: Government Printing Office.

Parker, William N. (1970), "Slavery and Economic Development: An Hypothesis and Some Evidence," Agricultural History, Vol. 44, pp. 115-125.

Pratten, C. and Dean, R. M. (1965), The Economics of Large-Scale Production in British Industry, Cambridge, England: Department of Applied Economics.

Raiffa, A. and Schlaiffer, R. (1961), Applied Statistical Decision Theory, Boston: Harvard University Press.

Randall, James G. and Donald, Douglas (1961), The Civil War and Reconstruction, Second Edition, Boston: D.C. Heath and Company.

Ransom, Roger and Sutch, Richard, "The Impact of the Civil War and Emancipation on Southern Agriculture," Southern Economic History Project, Working Paper Number 12 (mimeo).

Reynolds, A. R. (1957), The Daniel Shaw Lumber Company, New York: New York University Press.

Richardson, D. H. (1968), "The Exact Distribution of a Structural Coefficient Estimator," Journal of the American Statistical Association, Vol. 63, pp. 1214-1226.

Ringstad, V. (1974), "Some Empirical Evidence on the Decreasing Scale Elasticity," Econometrica, Vol. 42, pp. 87-102.

Rothbarth, E. (1946), "Causes of the Superior Efficiency of the U.S.A. Industry as Compared with British Industry," Economic Journal, Vol. 56, pp. 383-390.

Rosenberg, N. (1969), The American System of Manufacturers, Edinburgh: Edinburgh University Press.

Rosenberg, N., editor (1971), The Economics of Technological Change, London: Penguin Books.

Russel, Robert R. (1938), "The General Effects of Slavery upon Southern Economic Progress," Journal of Southern History, Vol. 4, pp. 34-54.

Sato, R. and Hoffman, R. F. (1968), "Production Functions with Variable Elasticity of Factor Substitution: Some Analysis and Testing," Review of Economics and Statistics, Vol. 50, pp. 453-460.

Saving, Thomas R. (1961), "Estimation of Optimum Size of Plant by the Survivor Technique," Quarterly Journal of Economics, Vol. 75, pp. 469-607.

Scherer, F. M. (March, 1974), "Economies of Scale and Industrial Concentration," paper presented to the Columbia Law School Conference on Industrial Concentration: The Economic Issues.

Schmidt, Louis B. (1920), "The Westward Movement of the Wheat Growing Industry in the United States," Iowa Journal of History and Politics, 18.

Sellers, James L. (1927), "The Economic Incidence of the Civil War in the South," Mississippi Valley Historical Review, Vol. 14.

Seventh Census (1859), "Statistics of Manufactures of the Seventh Census," Senate Executive Documents, 35 Cong., 2d sess.

Shepherd, William A. (1967), "What does the Survivor Technique show about Economies of Scale," Southern Economic Journal, Vol. 34, pp. 113-122.

Smiley, G. (1975), "Interest Rate Movements in the United States," Journal of Economic History, Vol. 35, pp. 591-620.

Smith, Caleb (1955), "Survey of the Empirical Evidence on Economies of Scale," Business Concentration and Price Policy, NBER, Princeton: Princeton University Press.

Smith, Hamilton (1850), "What the Southern and Western States Can Do in Competition with the North in Manufactures of Cotton," letter to A. A. Lawrence of Boston, Feb. 1, 1850. Reprinted in De Bow's Review, 8, pp. 550-555.

Solow, R. M., "Some Recent Developments in the Theory of Production," Murray Brown, editor, The Theory and Empirical Analysis of Production, NBER, Studies in Income and Wealth, Vol. 31, pp. 25-50.

Solow, R. M. (1960), "Investment and Technical Progress," Arrow, Karlin and suppes, editors, Mathematical Methods in the Social Sciences, Stanford: Stanford University Press, pp. 84-104.

Solow, R. M. (1957), "Technological Change and the Aggregate Production Function," The Review of Economics and Statistics, Vol. 39, pp. 312-320.

Soskice, David (1968), "A Modification of the CES Production Function to Allow for Changing Returns to Scale Over the Function," Review of Economics and Statistics, Vol. 50, pp. 446-448.

Stigler, George J. (1958), "The Economies of Scale," Journal of Law and Economics, pp. 54-71.

Stigler, George J. (1950), "Monopoly and Oligopoly my Merger," American Economic Review, suplement Vol. 04, pp. 23-34.

Stigler, George J., editor (1955), Business Concentration and Price Policy, NBER, Princeton: Princeton University Press.

Strassman, W. Paul (1959), Risk and Technological Innovation: American Manufacturing Methods During the Nineteenth Century, Ithaca: Cornell University Press.

Swisher, Jacob A. (1940), Iowa, Land of Many Mills, Iowa City: State Historical Society of Iowa.

Temin, Peter (1964), Iron and Steel in Nineteenth Century America: An Economic Inquiry, Cambridge, Massachusetts: M.I.T. Press.

Temin, Peter (1964), "A New Look at Hunter's Hypothesis About the Antebellum Iron Industry," American Economic Review, Vol. 54, pp. 344-351.

Temin, Peter (1966), "Labor Scarcity and the Problem of American Industrial Efficiency in the 1850's," Journal of Economic History, Vol. 26, pp. 277-298.

Temin, Peter (1968), "A Reply (to Ian M. Drummond)," Journal of Economic History, Vol. 28, pp. 124-125.

Temin, Peter (1971), "Labor Scarcity in America," *Journal of Interdisciplinary History*, 1.

Tenth Census (1883), *Report on the Manufactures of the United States at the Tenth Census*, Washington, D.C.: Government Printing Office.

Thiel, H. (1961), *Economic Forecasts and Policy*, Amsterdam: North-Holland.

Tiao, G. C. and Zellner, A. (1964), "Bayes' Theorem and the Use of Prior Knowledge in Regression Analysis," *Biometrika*, Vol. 51, pp. 219-230.

Tintner, G. (1955), "Stochastic Linear Programmilng with It's Applications to Agricultural Economics," Proceedings of the Second Symposium in Linear Programming, Washington, D.C., pp. 197-228.

Twelfth Census (1902), *Twelfth Census of the United States, 1900: Manufactures*, Washington, D.C.: Government Printing Office.

U.S. Bureau of the Census (1960), *Historical Statistics of the United States*, Colonial Times to 1957, Washington, D.C.: U.S. Government Printing Office.

U.S. Bureau of the Census (1967), *Concentration Ratios in Manufacturing Industry, 1963*, Senate Subcommittee on Antitrust and Monopoly of the Committee on the Judiciary, 90th Cong., 1s sess.

Uselding, Paul (1970), *Studies in the Technological Development of the American Economy During the First Half of the Nineteenth Century*, (Ph.D. Thesis, Northwestern University), New York: Arno Press.

Wagner, H. (1959), "Linear Programming Techniques for Regression Analysis," *Journal of the American Statistical Association*, Vol. 54, pp. 206-212.

Walsh, Margaret (1969), "The Manufacturing Frontier: Pioneer Industry in Antebellum Wisconsin, 1830-1860," (Ph.D. Thesis, University of Wisconsin), Ann Arbor: University Microfilms.

Walsh, Margaret (1972), *The Manufacturing Frontier*, Madison: State Historical Society of Wisconsin.

Walters, A. A. (1963), "Production and Cost Functions: An Econometric Survey," *Econometrica*, Vol. 31, pp. 1-66.

Week Report, supplement to *Tenth Census of the United States: 1880, Vol. XX, Report on the Statistics of Wages in Manufacturing Industry with Supplementary Reports*.

Weiss, Leonard (1964), "The Survival Technique and the Extent of Suboptimal Capacity," Journal of Political Economy, Vol. 72, pp. 246-261.

Weiss, Leonard (1965), "The Extent of Suboptimal Capacity: A Correction," Journal of Political Economy, Vol. 73, pp. 300-301.

Weiss, Leonard (1965), "T. R. Saving, the Four Parameter Lognormal Diseconomies of Scale and the Size Distribution of Manufacturing Establishments," International Economic Review, pp. 105-114.

Wilks, S. S. (1945), Mathematical Statistics, Princeton: Princeton University Press.

Williamson, Harold F., editor (1951), The Growth of the American Economy, Englewood Cliffs: Prentice-Hall, Inc., Second Edition.

Williamson, Jeffrey (1974), Late Nineteenth Century American Development: A General Equilibrium History, Cambridge: Cambridge University Press.

Williamson, Jeffrey (1975), "Railroads and Midwestern Development 1870-90," in D. C. Klingaman and Richard K. Vedder, Essays in Nineteenth Century Economic History, Athens: Ohio University Press.

Wolfe, P. (1959), "The Simplex Method for Quadratic Programming," Econometrica, Vol. 27, pp. 382-398.

Wright, C. C. (1900), The History and Growth of the United States Census, Washington, D.C.: Government Printing Office.

Yasuba, Y. (1961), "The Profitability and Viability of Plantation Slavery in the United States," Economic Studies Quarterly, Vol. 12, pp. 60-67.

Zellner, A.; Kmenta, J.; and Dreze, J. (1966), "Specification and Estimation of Cobb-Douglas Production Function Models," Econometrica, Vol. 34, pp. 784-795.

Zellner, A. and Revankar, N. S. (1969), "Generalized Production Functions," Review of Economic Studies, Vol. 36, pp. 241-250.

Zevin, Robert B. (1971), "The Growth of Cotton Textile Production After 1815," in Fogel and Engerman (eds.), The Reinterpretation of American Economic History, New York: Harper and Row.

Zevin, Robert B. (1975), The Growth of Manufacturing in Early Nineteenth Century New England, New York: Arno Press.

APPENDIX A

ORDINARY LEAST SQUARES ESTIMATES OF THE PRODUCTION FUNCTION
BY INDUSTRY, REGION AND YEAR

APPENDIX A.1

ORDINARY LEAST SQUARES ESTIMATES OF THE PRODUCTION FUNCTION FOR INDUSTRY SIC GROUP 20
CENSUS YEAR 1850
(T-RATIO)

REGION	INTERCEPT TERM	COEFFICIENT OF LABOR CAPITAL (1)	ECONOMIES OF SCALE (2)	F-RATIO	SAMPLE SIZE
MIDDLE ATLANTIC	3.21	.75* .43* (9.24) (8.39)	1.18* (2.62)	172.24	210.
NEW ENGLAND	1.84	.73* .57* (5.59) (5.22)	1.30* (2.97)	84.55	78.
PACIFIC	4.99	.06 .48* (.23) (3.33)	.54 (-1.85)	6.27	31.
SOUTHERN	3.79	.81* .33* (9.52) (5.92)	1.14* (1.97)	149.03	289.
WESTERN	2.49	.41* .60* (3.88) (8.28)	1.00 (.03)	102.24	176.
THE UNITED STATES	2.50	.64* .54* (12.63) (16.61)	1.17* (4.18)	505.29	784.

FOOTNOTES --
(1) THE COEFFICIENT IS COMPARED TO A VALUE OF ZERO FOR TESTS OF SIGNIFICANCE
(2) THE COEFFICIENT IS COMPARED TO A VALUE OF ONE FOR TESTS OF SIGNIFICANCE
*   COEFFICIENT SIGNIFICANTLY GREATER THAN ZERO (ONE) AT THE FIVE PERCENT LEVEL
** COEFFICIENT SIGNIFICANTLY LESS THAN ZERO (ONE) AT THE FIVE PERCENT LEVEL
REGIONS NOT APPEARING ABOVE MET ONE OF TWO CONDITIONS . . . .
   (1) SAMPLE SIZE SMALLER THAN TWELVE, OR
   (2) NO SAMPLE FOR THE REGION (SEE TABLE 3.1)
REGIONS AS DESCRIBED IN THE TEXT

APPENDIX A.2

ORDINARY LEAST SQUARES ESTIMATES OF THE PRODUCTION FUNCTION FOR INDUSTRY SIC GROUP 21
CENSUS YEAR 1850
(T-RATIO)

REGION	INTERCEPT TERM	COEFFICIENT OF LABOR CAPITAL (1)	ECONOMIES OF SCALE (2)	F-RATIO	SAMPLE SIZE
MIDDLE ATLANTIC	2.68	.42 .55* (2.06) (4.46)	.97 -.20 (-.20)	24.89	20.
SOUTHERN	1.35	.20 .72* (1.05) (4.27)	.92 (-.91)	64.93	27.
WESTERN	1.06	.01 .88 (.01) (1.92)	.88 (-.54)	8.45	13.
THE UNITED STATES	1.95	.19 .67** (1.64) (6.72)	.86** (-2.02)	94.73	64.

FOOTNOTES --
(1) THE COEFFICIENT IS COMPARED TO A VALUE OF ZERO FOR TESTS OF SIGNIFICANCE
(2) THE COEFFICIENT IS COMPARED TO A VALUE OF ONE FOR TESTS OF SIGNIFICANCE
*   COEFFICIENT SIGNIFICANTLY GREATER THAN ZERO (ONE) AT THE FIVE PERCENT LEVEL
** COEFFICIENT SIGNIFICANTLY LESS THAN ZERO (ONE) AT THE FIVE PERCENT LEVEL
REGIONS NOT APPEARING ABOVE MET ONE OF TWO CONDITIONS . . .
    (1) SAMPLE SIZE SMALLER THAN TWELVE, OR
    (2) NO SAMPLE FOR THE REGION (SEE TABLE 3.1)
REGIONS AS DESCRIBED IN THE TEXT

APPENDIX A.3

ORDINARY LEAST SQUARES ESTIMATES OF THE PRODUCTION FUNCTION FOR INDUSTRY SIC GROUP 22
CENSUS YEAR 1850
(T-RATIO)

REGION	INTERCEPT TERM	COEFFICIENT OF LABOR (1)	COEFFICIENT OF CAPITAL (1)	ECONOMIES OF SCALE (2)	F-RATIO	SAMPLE SIZE
MIDDLE ATLANTIC	2.49	.40* (3.14)	.52* (4.24)	.92 (-1.31)	117.16	31.
NEW ENGLAND	1.49	.33 (1.68)	.63* (3.33)	.96 (-.63)	116.10	53.
SOUTHERN	.88	.23 (1.92)	.71* (6.24)	.95 (-.84)	126.15	52.
WESTERN	1.63	.51* (3.47)	.60* (4.15)	1.11 (1.11)	63.11	29.
THE UNITED STATES	1.32	.30* (4.26)	.66* (9.59)	.96 (-1.27)	493.06	165.

FOOTNOTES --
(1) THE COEFFICIENT IS COMPARED TO A VALUE OF ZERO FOR TESTS OF SIGNIFICANCE
(2) THE COEFFICIENT IS COMPARED TO A VALUE OF ONE FOR TESTS OF SIGNIFICANCE
*   COEFFICIENT SIGNIFICANTLY GREATER THAN ZERO (ONE) AT THE FIVE PERCENT LEVEL
** COEFFICIENT SIGNIFICANTLY LESS THAN ZERO (ONE) AT THE FIVE PERCENT LEVEL
    REGIONS NOT APPEARING ABOVE MET ONE OF TWO CONDITIONS . . .
    (1) SAMPLE SIZE SMALLER THAN TWELVE, OR
    (2) NO SAMPLE FOR THE REGION (SEE TABLE 3.1)
    REGIONS AS DESCRIBED IN THE TEXT

APPENDIX A.4

ORDINARY LEAST SQUARES ESTIMATES OF THE PRODUCTION FUNCTION FOR INDUSTRY SIC GROUP 23
CENSUS YEAR 1850
(T-RATIO)

REGION	INTERCEPT TERM	COEFFICIENT OF LABOR (1)	COEFFICIENT OF CAPITAL (1)	ECONOMIES OF SCALE (2)	F-RATIO	SAMPLE SIZE
MIDDLE ATLANTIC	1.17	.33* (3.18)	.72* (7.70)	1.05 (.74)	128.78	78.
NEW ENGLAND	1.04	.31* (2.10)	.73* (5.10)	1.04 (.43)	58.62	41.
SOUTHERN	4.04	.66* (7.45)	.29* (4.48)	.95 (-.67)	88.70	122.
WESTERN	1.63	.26* (2.86)	.69* (10.63)	.95 (-.69)	110.77	80.
THE UNITED STATES	2.26	.44* (9.17)	.56* (13.75)	1.00 (-.08)	375.98	321.

FOOTNOTES --
(1) THE COEFFICIENT IS COMPARED TO A VALUE OF ZERO FOR TESTS OF SIGNIFICANCE
(2) THE COEFFICIENT IS COMPARED TO A VALUE OF ONE FOR TESTS OF SIGNIFICANCE
* COEFFICIENT SIGNIFICANTLY GREATER THAN ZERO (ONE) AT THE FIVE PERCENT LEVEL
** COEFFICIENT SIGNIFICANTLY LESS THAN ZERO (ONE) AT THE FIVE PERCENT LEVEL
REGIONS NOT APPEARING ABOVE MET ONE OF TWO CONDITIONS . . .
   (1) SAMPLE SIZE SMALLER THAN TWELVE, OR
   (2) NO SAMPLE FOR THE REGION (SEE TABLE 3.1)
REGIONS AS DESCRIBED IN THE TEXT

APPENDIX A.5

ORDINARY LEAST SQUARES ESTIMATES OF THE PRODUCTION FUNCTION FOR INDUSTRY SIC GROUP 24
CENSUS YEAR 1850
(T-RATIO)

REGION	INTERCEPT TERM	COEFFICIENT OF LABOR CAPITAL (1)	ECONOMIES OF SCALE (2)	F-RATIO	SAMPLE SIZE
MIDDLE ATLANTIC	1.21	.28* .71* (3.22) (9.43)	.99 (-.19)	142.81	142.
NEW ENGLAND	1.86	.43* .60* (6.25) (10.27)	1.03 (.68)	318.46	181.
PACIFIC	-.41	.08 1.02* (.43) (7.22)	1.10 (.64)	39.89	46.
SOUTHERN	1.91	.56* .59* (8.37) (11.88)	1.14* (3.10)	371.43	396.
WESTERN	2.26	.43* .57* (6.16) (10.46)	.99 (-.11)	190.29	268.
THE UNITED STATES	.88	.37* .75* (10.29) (28.07)	1.12* (4.68)	1257.53	1033.

FOOTNOTES --
(1) THE COEFFICIENT IS COMPARED TO A VALUE OF ZERO FOR TESTS OF SIGNIFICANCE
(2) THE COEFFICIENT IS COMPARED TO A VALUE OF ONE FOR TESTS OF SIGNIFICANCE
* COEFFICIENT SIGNIFICANTLY GREATER THAN ZERO (ONE) AT THE FIVE PERCENT LEVEL
** COEFFICIENT SIGNIFICANTLY LESS THAN ZERO (ONE) AT THE FIVE PERCENT LEVEL
REGIONS NOT APPEARING ABOVE MET ONE OF TWO CONDITIONS . . .
    (1) SAMPLE SIZE SMALLER THAN TWELVE, OR
    (2) NO SAMPLE FOR THE REGION (SEE TABLE 3.1)
REGIONS AS DESCRIBED IN THE TEXT

APPENDIX A.6

ORDINARY LEAST SQUARES ESTIMATES OF THE PRODUCTION FUNCTION FOR INDUSTRY SIC GROUP 25
CENSUS YEAR 1850
(T-RATIO)

REGION	INTERCEPT TERM	COEFFICIENT OF LABOR CAPITAL (1)	ECONOMIES OF SCALE (2)	F-RATIO	SAMPLE SIZE
MIDDLE ATLANTIC	-.83	-.28 1.10* (-1.33) (6.24)	.82 (-1.48)	41.61	49.
NEW ENGLAND	2.88	.50* .51* (4.58) (4.15)	1.00 (.03)	188.06	20.
SOUTHERN	2.63	.41* .58* (3.03) (6.31)	.98 (-.18)	86.80	82.
WESTERN	.79	.06 .88* (.45) (7.93)	.94 (-.98)	157.95	59.
THE UNITED STATES	1.15	.09 .82* (1.04) (13.10)	.90 (-1.93)	259.35	214.

FOOTNOTES --
(1) THE COEFFICIENT IS COMPARED TO A VALUE OF ZERO FOR TESTS OF SIGNIFICANCE
(2) THE COEFFICIENT IS COMPARED TO A VALUE OF ONE FOR TESTS OF SIGNIFICANCE
* COEFFICIENT SIGNIFICANTLY GREATER THAN ZERO (ONE) AT THE FIVE PERCENT LEVEL
** COEFFICIENT SIGNIFICANTLY LESS THAN ZERO (ONE) AT THE FIVE PERCENT LEVEL
REGIONS NOT APPEARING ABOVE MET ONE OF TWO CONDITIONS . . .
(1) SAMPLE SIZE SMALLER THAN TWELVE, OR
(2) NO SAMPLE FOR THE REGION (SEE TABLE 3.1)
REGIONS AS DESCRIBED IN THE TEXT

APPENDIX A.7

ORDINARY LEAST SQUARES ESTIMATES OF THE PRODUCTION FUNCTION FOR INDUSTRY SIC GROUP 28
CENSUS YEAR 1850
(T-RATIO)

REGION	INTERCEPT TERM	COEFFICIENT OF LABOR CAPITAL (1)	ECONOMIES OF SCALE (2)	F-RATIO	SAMPLE SIZE
MIDDLE ATLANTIC	3.02	.26 (.62) .49 (1.41)	.75 (-1.09)	6.40	12.
NEW ENGLAND	2.52	.54* (2.79) .50* (2.97)	1.04 (.31)	41.20	16.
WESTERN	3.69	.73* (5.21) .40* (4.68)	1.13 (1.03)	48.81	25.
THE UNITED STATES	3.33	.43* (3.74) .44* (5.23)	.87 (-1.63)	71.90	63.

FOOTNOTES --
(1) THE COEFFICIENT IS COMPARED TO A VALUE OF ZERO FOR TESTS OF SIGNIFICANCE
(2) THE COEFFICIENT IS COMPARED TO A VALUE OF ONE FOR TESTS OF SIGNIFICANCE
*   COEFFICIENT SIGNIFICANTLY GREATER THAN ZERO (ONE) AT THE FIVE PERCENT LEVEL
** COEFFICIENT SIGNIFICANTLY LESS THAN ZERO (ONE) AT THE FIVE PERCENT LEVEL
REGIONS NOT APPEARING ABOVE MET ONE OF TWO CONDITIONS . . .
    (1) SAMPLE SIZE SMALLER THAN TWELVE, OR
    (2) NO SAMPLE FOR THE REGION (SEE TABLE 3.1)
REGIONS AS DESCRIBED IN THE TEXT

APPENDIX A.8

ORDINARY LEAST SQUARES ESTIMATES OF THE PRODUCTION FUNCTION FOR INDUSTRY SIC GROUP 31
CENSUS YEAR 1850
(T-RATIO)

REGION	INTERCEPT TERM	COEFFICIENT OF LABOR CAPITAL (1) (1)	ECONOMIES OF SCALE (2)	F-RATIO	SAMPLE SIZE
MIDDLE ATLANTIC	3.94	.67* .33* (13.35) (8.97)	1.01 (.18)	367.53	245.
NEW ENGLAND	2.70	.45* .53* (10.13) (12.68)	.97 (-.99)	614.52	225.
SOUTHERN	3.40	.56* .42* (9.33) (10.57)	.98 (-.32)	244.50	396.
WESTERN	3.88	.74* .34* (10.33) (5.74)	1.08 (1.29)	164.09	182.
THE UNITED STATES	3.52	.58* .40* (21.57) (18.64)	.98 (-.84)	1283.96	1048.

FOOTNOTES --
(1) THE COEFFICIENT IS COMPARED TO A VALUE OF ZERO FOR TESTS OF SIGNIFICANCE
(2) THE COEFFICIENT IS COMPARED TO A VALUE OF ONE FOR TESTS OF SIGNIFICANCE
* COEFFICIENT SIGNIFICANTLY GREATER THAN ZERO (ONE) AT THE FIVE PERCENT LEVEL
** COEFFICIENT SIGNIFICANTLY LESS THAN ZERO (ONE) AT THE FIVE PERCENT LEVEL
REGIONS NOT APPEARING ABOVE MET ONE OF TWO CONDITIONS . . .
    (1) SAMPLE SIZE SMALLER THAN TWELVE, OR
    (2) NO SAMPLE FOR THE REGION (SEE TABLE 3.1)
REGIONS AS DESCRIBED IN THE TEXT

218

APPENDIX A.9

ORDINARY LEAST SQUARES ESTIMATES OF THE PRODUCTION FUNCTION FOR INDUSTRY SIC GROUP 33
CENSUS YEAR 1850
(T-RATIO)

REGION	INTERCEPT TERM	COEFFICIENT OF LABOR CAPITAL (1)	ECONOMIES OF SCALE (2)	F-RATIO	SAMPLE SIZE
MIDDLE ATLANTIC	4.80	.39 .28 (1.62) (1.28)	-.68** (-3.64)	29.64	23.
NEW ENGLAND	4.44	.64* .27 (2.20) (.93)	.91 (-1.03)	57.60	23.
SOUTHERN	3.24	.23 .51* (.98) (2.86)	.74** (-2.77)	49.22	41.
WESTERN	4.13	.64* .29 (2.77) (1.48)	.93 (-.40)	15.38	18.
THE UNITED STATES	3.90	.41* .38* (3.96) (4.17)	.79** (-4.33)	144.35	106.

FOOTNOTES --
(1) THE COEFFICIENT IS COMPARED TO A VALUE OF ZERO FOR TESTS OF SIGNIFICANCE
(2) THE COEFFICIENT IS COMPARED TO A VALUE OF ONE FOR TESTS OF SIGNIFICANCE
* COEFFICIENT SIGNIFICANTLY GREATER THAN ZERO (ONE) AT THE FIVE PERCENT LEVEL
** COEFFICIENT SIGNIFICANTLY LESS THAN ZERO (ONE) AT THE FIVE PERCENT LEVEL
REGIONS NOT APPEARING ABOVE MET ONE OF TWO CONDITIONS . . .
   (1) SAMPLE SIZE SMALLER THAN TWELVE, OR
   (2) NO SAMPLE FOR THE REGION (SEE TABLE 3.1)
REGIONS AS DESCRIBED IN THE TEXT

APPENDIX A.10

ORDINARY LEAST SQUARES ESTIMATES OF THE PRODUCTION FUNCTION FOR INDUSTRY SIC GROUP 34
CENSUS YEAR 1850
(T-RATIO)

REGION	INTERCEPT TERM	COEFFICIENT OF LABOR CAPITAL (1)	ECONOMIES OF SCALE (2)	F-RATIO	SAMPLE SIZE
MIDDLE ATLANTIC	5.55	.92* (4.40)	.10 (.63)	1.02 (.20)	94.86	38.
NEW ENGLAND	2.12	.47* (2.85)	.60* (3.99)	1.07 (.80)	74.20	41.
SOUTHERN	2.00	.44* (2.35)	.66* (5.81)	1.10 (.80)	67.74	46.
WESTERN	2.99	.72* (4.12)	.46* (3.91)	1.18 (1.53)	62.65	47.
THE UNITED STATES	.92	.12 (1.49)	.83* (15.67)	.95 (-.99)	303.11	183.

FOOTNOTES --
(1) THE COEFFICIENT IS COMPARED TO A VALUE OF ZERO FOR TESTS OF SIGNIFICANCE
(2) THE COEFFICIENT IS COMPARED TO A VALUE OF ONE FOR TESTS OF SIGNIFICANCE
* COEFFICIENT SIGNIFICANTLY GREATER THAN ZERO (ONE) AT THE FIVE PERCENT LEVEL
** COEFFICIENT SIGNIFICANTLY LESS THAN ZERO (ONE) AT THE FIVE PERCENT LEVEL
REGIONS NOT APPEARING ABOVE MET ONE OF TWO CONDITIONS . . .
   (1) SAMPLE SIZE SMALLER THAN TWELVE, OR
   (2) NO SAMPLE FOR THE REGION (SEE TABLE 3.1)
REGIONS AS DESCRIBED IN THE TEXT

APPENDIX A.11

ORDINARY LEAST SQUARES ESTIMATES OF THE PRODUCTION FUNCTION FOR INDUSTRY SIC GROUP 35
CENSUS YEAR 1850
(T-RATIO)

REGION	INTERCEPT TERM	COEFFICIENT OF LABOR CAPITAL (1)	ECONOMIES OF SCALE (2)	F-RATIO	SAMPLE SIZE
MIDDLE ATLANTIC	2.01	.11 .70* (.46) (2.71)	.81 (-2.03)	39.40	18.
NEW ENGLAND	1.90	.35 .64* (2.01) (4.11)	.99 (-.19)	164.26	25.
SOUTHERN	2.01	.07 .70 (.17) (2.05)	.76 (-1.54)	17.65	19.
THE UNITED STATES	1.99	.22 .67* (1.71) (5.63)	.89** (-2.44)	221.18	71.

FOOTNOTES --
(1) THE COEFFICIENT IS COMPARED TO A VALUE OF ZERO FOR TESTS OF SIGNIFICANCE
(2) THE COEFFICIENT IS COMPARED TO A VALUE OF ONE FOR TESTS OF SIGNIFICANCE
* COEFFICIENT SIGNIFICANTLY GREATER THAN ZERO (ONE) AT THE FIVE PERCENT LEVEL
** COEFFICIENT SIGNIFICANTLY LESS THAN ZERO (ONE) AT THE FIVE PERCENT LEVEL
REGIONS NOT APPEARING ABOVE MET ONE OF TWO CONDITIONS . . .
  (1) SAMPLE SIZE SMALLER THAN TWELVE, OR
  (2) NO SAMPLE FOR THE REGION (SEE TABLE 3.1)
REGIONS AS DESCRIBED IN THE TEXT

APPENDIX A.12

ORDINARY LEAST SQUARES ESTIMATES OF THE PRODUCTION FUNCTION FOR INDUSTRY SIC GROUP 37
CENSUS YEAR 1850
(T-RATIO)

REGION	INTERCEPT TERM	COEFFICIENT OF LABOR (1)	COEFFICIENT OF CAPITAL (1)	ECONOMIES OF SCALE (2)	F-RATIO	SAMPLE SIZE
MIDDLE ATLANTIC	-.07	.05 (.41)	.94* (8.55)	.99 (-.14)	168.32	58.
NEW ENGLAND	4.06	.70* (3.97)	.33* (2.64)	1.02 (.23)	78.00	33.
SOUTHERN	2.57	.40* (4.48)	.59* (9.60)	.99 (-.26)	265.46	104.
WESTERN	1.06	.43 (1.88)	.73* (3.80)	1.16 (1.39)	56.59	41.
THE UNITED STATES	2.41	.39* (5.72)	.59* (11.08)	.98 (-.53)	488.76	236.

FOOTNOTES --
(1) THE COEFFICIENT IS COMPARED TO A VALUE OF ZERO FOR TESTS OF SIGNIFICANCE
(2) THE COEFFICIENT IS COMPARED TO A VALUE OF ONE FOR TESTS OF SIGNIFICANCE
 * COEFFICIENT SIGNIFICANTLY GREATER THAN ZERO (ONE) AT THE FIVE PERCENT LEVEL
 ** COEFFICIENT SIGNIFICANTLY LESS THAN ZERO (ONE) AT THE FIVE PERCENT LEVEL
REGIONS NOT APPEARING ABOVE MET ONE OF TWO CONDITIONS . . .
    (1) SAMPLE SIZE SMALLER THAN TWELVE, OR
    (2) NO SAMPLE FOR THE REGION (SEE TABLE 3.1)
REGIONS AS DESCRIBED IN THE TEXT

APPENDIX A.13

ORDINARY LEAST SQUARES ESTIMATES OF THE PRODUCTION FUNCTION FOR INDUSTRY SIC GROUP 20
CENSUS YEAR 1860
(T-RATIO)

REGION	INTERCEPT TERM	COEFFICIENT OF LABOR CAPITAL (1)	ECONOMIES OF SCALE (2)	F-RATIO	SAMPLE SIZE
MIDDLE ATLANTIC	2.65	.67* (6.73) .52* (8.14)	1.20* (2.56)	156.48	218.
NEW ENGLAND	1.22	.48* (4.01) .71* (8.02)	1.19 (1.86)	83.20	95.
PACIFIC	3.83	.75* (4.18) .44* (4.01)	1.19 (1.17)	29.85	96.
SOUTHERN	2.62	.70* (11.07) .51* (12.83)	1.22* (4.30)	361.02	444.
WESTERN	3.07	.56* (6.91) .49* (9.62)	1.05 (.81)	186.06	302.
THE UNITED STATES	2.39	.62* (15.09) .56* (21.78)	1.18* (5.72)	907.44	1155.

FOOTNOTES --
(1) THE COEFFICIENT IS COMPARED TO A VALUE OF ZERO FOR TESTS OF SIGNIFICANCE
(2) THE COEFFICIENT IS COMPARED TO A VALUE OF ONE FOR TESTS OF SIGNIFICANCE
* COEFFICIENT SIGNIFICANTLY GREATER THAN ZERO (ONE) AT THE FIVE PERCENT LEVEL
** COEFFICIENT SIGNIFICANTLY LESS THAN ZERO (ONE) AT THE FIVE PERCENT LEVEL
REGIONS NOT APPEARING ABOVE MET ONE OF TWO CONDITIONS . . .
  (1) SAMPLE SIZE SMALLER THAN TWELVE, OR
  (2) NO SAMPLE FOR THE REGION (SEE TABLE 3.1)
REGIONS AS DESCRIBED IN THE TEXT

APPENDIX A.14

ORDINARY LEAST SQUARES ESTIMATES OF THE PRODUCTION FUNCTION FOR INDUSTRY SIC GROUP 21
CENSUS YEAR 1860
(T-RATIO)

REGION	INTERCEPT TERM	COEFFICIENT OF LABOR CAPITAL (1)	COEFFICIENT OF CAPITAL (1)	ECONOMIES OF SCALE (2)	F-RATIO	SAMPLE SIZE
MIDDLE ATLANTIC	1.61	.34 (1.57)	.73* (3.52)	1.07 (.51)	32.01	21.
SOUTHERN	2.53	.44* (2.45)	.52* (3.67)	.96 (-.41)	62.05	28.
WESTERN	.65	.14 (.54)	.81* (3.15)	.95 (-.30)	20.78	17.
THE UNITED STATES	1.53	.14 (1.30)	.73* (7.31)	.87** (-2.51)	147.05	74.

FOOTNOTES --
(1) THE COEFFICIENT IS COMPARED TO A VALUE OF ZERO FOR TESTS OF SIGNIFICANCE
(2) THE COEFFICIENT IS COMPARED TO A VALUE OF ONE FOR TESTS OF SIGNIFICANCE
* COEFFICIENT SIGNIFICANTLY GREATER THAN ZERO (ONE) AT THE FIVE PERCENT LEVEL
** COEFFICIENT SIGNIFICANTLY LESS THAN ZERO (ONE) AT THE FIVE PERCENT LEVEL
REGIONS NOT APPEARING ABOVE MET ONE OF TWO CONDITIONS . . .
    (1) SAMPLE SIZE SMALLER THAN TWELVE, OR
    (2) NO SAMPLE FOR THE REGION (SEE TABLE 3.1)
REGIONS AS DESCRIBED IN THE TEXT

APPENDIX A.15

ORDINARY LEAST SQUARES ESTIMATES OF THE PRODUCTION FUNCTION FOR INDUSTRY SIC GROUP 22
CENSUS YEAR 1860
(T-RATIO)

REGION	INTERCEPT TERM	COEFFICIENT OF LABOR (1)	COEFFICIENT OF CAPITAL (1)	ECONOMIES OF SCALE (2)	F-RATIO	SAMPLE SIZE
MIDDLE ATLANTIC	2.61	.44 (1.59)	.51 (1.92)	.95 (-.56)	69.23	20.
NEW ENGLAND	1.29	.34* (2.05)	.68* (3.72)	1.02 (.38)	135.16	39.
SOUTHERN	1.15	.18 (1.17)	.73* (4.50)	.91 (-1.37)	98.67	39.
WESTERN	3.16	.99* (3.72)	.35 (1.87)	1.35* (2.28)	46.02	27.
THE UNITED STATES	1.80	.40* (4.64)	.61* (6.86)	1.00 (.13)	389.20	127.

FOOTNOTES --
(1) THE COEFFICIENT IS COMPARED TO A VALUE OF ZERO FOR TESTS OF SIGNIFICANCE
(2) THE COEFFICIENT IS COMPARED TO A VALUE OF ONE FOR TESTS OF SIGNIFICANCE
* COEFFICIENT SIGNIFICANTLY GREATER THAN ZERO (ONE) AT THE FIVE PERCENT LEVEL
** COEFFICIENT SIGNIFICANTLY LESS THAN ZERO (ONE) AT THE FIVE PERCENT LEVEL
REGIONS NOT APPEARING ABOVE MET ONE OF TWO CONDITIONS . . .
    (1) SAMPLE SIZE SMALLER THAN TWELVE, OR
    (2) NO SAMPLE FOR THE REGION (SEE TABLE 3.1)
REGIONS AS DESCRIBED IN THE TEXT

APPENDIX A.16

ORDINARY LEAST SQUARES ESTIMATES OF THE PRODUCTION FUNCTION FOR INDUSTRY SIC GROUP 23
CENSUS YEAR 1860
(T-RATIO)

REGION	INTERCEPT TERM	COEFFICIENT OF LABOR CAPITAL (1) (1)	ECONOMIES OF SCALE (2)	F-RATIO	SAMPLE SIZE
MIDDLE ATLANTIC	1.69	.29* .67* (3.67) (9.28)	.96 (-.71)	205.01	93.
NEW ENGLAND	.91	.28* .77* (3.75) (9.21)	1.05 (.93)	170.50	54.
SOUTHERN	2.77	.43* .50* (4.03) (5.81)	.93 (-.79)	60.92	74.
WESTERN	1.21	.22* .76* (2.25) (9.68)	.98 (-.25)	112.92	74.
THE UNITED STATES	1.80	.32* .66* (7.41) (16.53)	.97 (-.86)	504.26	301.

FOOTNOTES --
(1) THE COEFFICIENT IS COMPARED TO A VALUE OF ZERO FOR TESTS OF SIGNIFICANCE
(2) THE COEFFICIENT IS COMPARED TO A VALUE OF ONE FOR TESTS OF SIGNIFICANCE
*   COEFFICIENT SIGNIFICANTLY GREATER THAN ZERO (ONE) AT THE FIVE PERCENT LEVEL
** COEFFICIENT SIGNIFICANTLY LESS THAN ZERO (ONE) AT THE FIVE PERCENT LEVEL
    REGIONS NOT APPEARING ABOVE MET ONE OF TWO CONDITIONS . . .
    (1) SAMPLE SIZE SMALLER THAN TWELVE, OR
    (2) NO SAMPLE FOR THE REGION (SEE TABLE 3.1)
    REGIONS AS DESCRIBED IN THE TEXT

APPENDIX A.17

ORDINARY LEAST SQUARES ESTIMATES OF THE PRODUCTION FUNCTION FOR INDUSTRY SIC GROUP 24
CENSUS YEAR 1860
(T-RATIO)

REGION	INTERCEPT TERM	COEFFICIENT OF LABOR CAPITAL (1)	ECONOMIES OF SCALE (2)	F-RATIO	SAMPLE SIZE
MIDDLE ATLANTIC	1.75	.49* .61* (6.61) (8.73)	1.10 (1.94)	220.57	146.
NEW ENGLAND	.73	.39* .74* (4.42) (9.48)	1.13* (2.80)	332.46	202.
PACIFIC	-1.95	.11 1.16* (1.24) (13.89)	1.27* (3.58)	181.27	172.
SOUTHERN	2.47	.60* .53* (11.16) (11.57)	1.14* (4.16)	639.47	447.
WESTERN	3.14	.73* .43* (11.85) (9.08)	1.16* (3.68)	380.45	425.
THE UNITED STATES	1.66	.51* .64* (16.16) (23.81)	1.15* (7.29)	1626.42	1392.

FOOTNOTES --
(1) THE COEFFICIENT IS COMPARED TO A VALUE OF ZERO FOR TESTS OF SIGNIFICANCE
(2) THE COEFFICIENT IS COMPARED TO A VALUE OF ONE FOR TESTS OF SIGNIFICANCE
* COEFFICIENT SIGNIFICANTLY GREATER THAN ZERO (ONE) AT THE FIVE PERCENT LEVEL
** COEFFICIENT SIGNIFICANTLY LESS THAN ZERO (ONE) AT THE FIVE PERCENT LEVEL
REGIONS NOT APPEARING ABOVE MET ONE OF TWO CONDITIONS . . .
  (1) SAMPLE SIZE SMALLER THAN TWELVE, OR
  (2) NO SAMPLE FOR THE REGION (SEE TABLE 3.1)
REGIONS AS DESCRIBED IN THE TEXT

APPENDIX A.18

ORDINARY LEAST SQUARES ESTIMATES OF THE PRODUCTION FUNCTION FOR INDUSTRY SIC GROUP 25
CENSUS YEAR 1860
(T-RATIO)

REGION	INTERCEPT TERM	COEFFICIENT OF LABOR CAPITAL (1)	ECONOMIES OF SCALE (2)	F-RATIO	SAMPLE SIZE
MIDDLE ATLANTIC	2.26	.36 .61* (1.96) (3.69)	.98 (-.22)	39.39	39.
NEW ENGLAND	-.92	.04 1.06* (.17) (4.04)	1.11 (.74)	30.34	24.
PACIFIC	-1.73	.01 1.17* (.06) (8.01)	1.18 (1.20)	41.36	16.
SOUTHERN	4.38	.61* .27 (3.04) (1.87)	.88 (-.88)	24.74	38.
WESTERN	2.42	.32* .60* (2.39) (5.76)	.92 (-.96)	69.08	66.
THE UNITED STATES	2.01	.30* .65* (3.87) (10.12)	.95 (-.87)	202.72	183.

FOOTNOTES --
(1) THE COEFFICIENT IS COMPARED TO A VALUE OF ZERO FOR TESTS OF SIGNIFICANCE
(2) THE COEFFICIENT IS COMPARED TO A VALUE OF ONE FOR TESTS OF SIGNIFICANCE
* COEFFICIENT SIGNIFICANTLY GREATER THAN ZERO (ONE) AT THE FIVE PERCENT LEVEL
** COEFFICIENT SIGNIFICANTLY LESS THAN ZERO (ONE) AT THE FIVE PERCENT LEVEL
REGIONS NOT APPEARING ABOVE MET ONE OF TWO CONDITIONS . . .
  (1) SAMPLE SIZE SMALLER THAN TWELVE, OR
  (2) NO SAMPLE FOR THE REGION (SEE TABLE 3.1)
REGIONS AS DESCRIBED IN THE TEXT

APPENDIX A.19

ORDINARY LEAST SQUARES ESTIMATES OF THE PRODUCTION FUNCTION FOR INDUSTRY SIC GROUP 28
CENSUS YEAR 1860
(T-RATIO)

REGION	INTERCEPT TERM	COEFFICIENT OF LABOR CAPITAL (1)	ECONOMIES OF SCALE (2)	F-RATIO	SAMPLE SIZE
MIDDLE ATLANTIC	.74	-.01 .81* (-.02) (5.03)	.80 (-1.41)	42.96	14.
NEW ENGLAND	2.06	.21 .63* (.61) (2.59)	.85 (-1.00)	35.66	12.
THE UNITED STATES	2.92	.41* .51* (2.78) (5.34)	.92 (-.98)	112.35	45.

FOOTNOTES --
(1) THE COEFFICIENT IS COMPARED TO A VALUE OF ZERO FOR TESTS OF SIGNIFICANCE
(2) THE COEFFICIENT IS COMPARED TO A VALUE OF ONE FOR TESTS OF SIGNIFICANCE
*   COEFFICIENT SIGNIFICANTLY GREATER THAN ZERO (ONE) AT THE FIVE PERCENT LEVEL
**   COEFFICIENT SIGNIFICANTLY LESS THAN ZERO (ONE) AT THE FIVE PERCENT LEVEL
.   REGIONS NOT APPEARING ABOVE MET ONE OF TWO CONDITIONS . . .
     (1) SAMPLE SIZE SMALLER THAN TWELVE, OR
     (2) NO SAMPLE FOR THE REGION (SEE TABLE 3.1)
     REGIONS AS DESCRIBED IN THE TEXT

APPENDIX A.20

ORDINARY LEAST SQUARES ESTIMATES OF THE PRODUCTION FUNCTION FOR INDUSTRY SIC GROUP 31
CENSUS YEAR 1860
(T-RATIO)

REGION	INTERCEPT TERM	COEFFICIENT OF LABOR CAPITAL (1) (1)	ECONOMIES OF SCALE (2)	F-RATIO	SAMPLE SIZE
MIDDLE ATLANTIC	3.56	.60* .42* (9.59) (9.57)	1.02 (.55)	425.24	206.
NEW ENGLAND	2.89	.49* .49* (6.48) (7.25)	.99 (-.33)	325.81	150.
PACIFIC	4.54	.75* .36* (3.77) (3.59)	1.11 (.72)	37.85	71.
SOUTHERN	4.25	.81* .28* (12.90) (6.67)	1.09* (2.04)	299.17	310.
WESTERN	3.91	.74* .35* (9.86) (7.25)	1.09 (1.68)	251.48	224.
THE UNITED STATES	3.54	.58* .42* (17.74) (17.10)	1.00 (-.19)	1298.35	961.

FOOTNOTES --
(1) THE COEFFICIENT IS COMPARED TO A VALUE OF ZERO FOR TESTS OF SIGNIFICANCE
(2) THE COEFFICIENT IS COMPARED TO A VALUE OF ONE FOR TESTS OF SIGNIFICANCE
*   COEFFICIENT SIGNIFICANTLY GREATER THAN ZERO (ONE) AT THE FIVE PERCENT LEVEL
** COEFFICIENT SIGNIFICANTLY LESS THAN ZERO (ONE) AT THE FIVE PERCENT LEVEL
    REGIONS NOT APPEARING ABOVE MET ONE OF TWO CONDITIONS . . .
    (1) SAMPLE SIZE SMALLER THAN TWELVE, OR
    (2) NO SAMPLE FOR THE REGION (SEE TABLE 3.1)
    REGIONS AS DESCRIBED IN THE TEXT

APPENDIX A.21

ORDINARY LEAST SQUARES ESTIMATES OF THE PRODUCTION FUNCTION FOR INDUSTRY SIC GROUP 33
CENSUS YEAR 1860
(T-RATIO)

REGION	INTERCEPT TERM	COEFFICIENT OF LABOR CAPITAL (1)	ECONOMIES OF SCALE (2)	F-RATIO	SAMPLE SIZE
MIDDLE ATLANTIC	3.98	.64* .34 (2.96) (1.83)	.98 (-.35)	110.05	32.
NEW ENGLAND	1.72	.41* .64* (2.74) (4.76)	1.05 (.84)	160.08	20.
SOUTHERN	3.70	.21 .53* (.98) (2.53)	-.73** (-2.08)	16.90	24.
WESTERN	6.59	.55 .09 (1.53) (.31)	.64 (-1.88)	5.89	16.
THE UNITED STATES	3.56	.46* .44* (3.92) (4.15)	-.90** (-2.10)	174.89	97.

FOOTNOTES --
(1) THE COEFFICIENT IS COMPARED TO A VALUE OF ZERO FOR TESTS OF SIGNIFICANCE
(2) THE COEFFICIENT IS COMPARED TO A VALUE OF ONE FOR TESTS OF SIGNIFICANCE
*   COEFFICIENT SIGNIFICANTLY GREATER THAN ZERO (ONE) AT THE FIVE PERCENT LEVEL
** COEFFICIENT SIGNIFICANTLY LESS THAN ZERO (ONE) AT THE FIVE PERCENT LEVEL
REGIONS NOT APPEARING ABOVE MET ONE OF TWO CONDITIONS . . .
    (1) SAMPLE SIZE SMALLER THAN TWELVE, OR
    (2) NO SAMPLE FOR THE REGION (SEE TABLE 3.1)
REGIONS AS DESCRIBED IN THE TEXT

APPENDIX A.22

ORDINARY LEAST SQUARES ESTIMATES OF THE PRODUCTION FUNCTION FOR INDUSTRY SIC GROUP 34
CENSUS YEAR 1860
(T-RATIO)

REGION	INTERCEPT TERM	COEFFICIENT OF LABOR (1)	COEFFICIENT OF CAPITAL (1)	ECONOMIES OF SCALE (2)	F-RATIO	SAMPLE SIZE
MIDDLE ATLANTIC	3.74	.62* (5.40)	.39* (3.98)	1.02 (.38)	310.53	50.
NEW ENGLAND	1.12	.29 (1.84)	.74* (5.45)	1.04 (.49)	120.02	50.
PACIFIC	-2.96	-.07 (-.24)	1.35* (4.18)	1.28 (.87)	10.66	12.
SOUTHERN	1.00	.09 (.85)	.84* (10.71)	.93 (-1.15)	221.46	80.
WESTERN	2.26	.41* (3.97)	.60* (7.11)	1.01 (.14)	118.56	103.
THE UNITED STATES	1.80	.29* (5.18)	.68* (14.77)	.98 (-.70)	650.97	295.

FOOTNOTES --
(1) THE COEFFICIENT IS COMPARED TO A VALUE OF ZERO FOR TESTS OF SIGNIFICANCE
(2) THE COEFFICIENT IS COMPARED TO A VALUE OF ONE FOR TESTS OF SIGNIFICANCE
* COEFFICIENT SIGNIFICANTLY GREATER THAN ZERO (ONE) AT THE FIVE PERCENT LEVEL
** COEFFICIENT SIGNIFICANTLY LESS THAN ZERO (ONE) AT THE FIVE PERCENT LEVEL
REGIONS NOT APPEARING ABOVE MET ONE OF TWO CONDITIONS . . .
  (1) SAMPLE SIZE SMALLER THAN TWELVE, OR
  (2) NO SAMPLE FOR THE REGION (SEE TABLE 3.1)
REGIONS AS DESCRIBED IN THE TEXT

APPENDIX A.23

ORDINARY LEAST SQUARES ESTIMATES OF THE PRODUCTION FUNCTION FOR INDUSTRY SIC GROUP 35
CENSUS YEAR 1860
(T-RATIO)

REGION	INTERCEPT TERM	COEFFICIENT OF LABOR CAPITAL (1)	ECONOMIES OF SCALE (2)	F-RATIO	SAMPLE SIZE
MIDDLE ATLANTIC	3.67	.35 .45 (.44) (.67)	.80 (-.93)	11.58	14.
NEW ENGLAND	3.25	.63* .45 (2.78) (2.05)	1.08 (1.08)	112.45	23.
SOUTHERN	1.46	.38 .73* (1.88) (5.25)	1.11 (1.36)	254.41	16.
WESTERN	1.46	.20 .76* (.73) (3.88)	.95 (-.36)	54.48	13.
THE UNITED STATES	1.70	.27 .71* (1.67) (5.59)	.98 (-.32)	192.61	73.

FOOTNOTES --
(1) THE COEFFICIENT IS COMPARED TO A VALUE OF ZERO FOR TESTS OF SIGNIFICANCE
(2) THE COEFFICIENT IS COMPARED TO A VALUE OF ONE FOR TESTS OF SIGNIFICANCE
* COEFFICIENT SIGNIFICANTLY GREATER THAN ZERO (ONE) AT THE FIVE PERCENT LEVEL
** COEFFICIENT SIGNIFICANTLY LESS THAN ZERO (ONE) AT THE FIVE PERCENT LEVEL
REGIONS NOT APPEARING ABOVE MET ONE OF TWO CONDITIONS . . .
(1) SAMPLE SIZE SMALLER THAN TWELVE, OR
(2) NO SAMPLE FOR THE REGION (SEE TABLE 3.1)
REGIONS AS DESCRIBED IN THE TEXT

APPENDIX A.24

ORDINARY LEAST SQUARES ESTIMATES OF THE PRODUCTION FUNCTION FOR INDUSTRY SIC GROUP 37
CENSUS YEAR 1860
(T-RATIO)

REGION	INTERCEPT TERM	COEFFICIENT OF LABOR CAPITAL (1)	COEFFICIENT OF CAPITAL (1)	ECONOMIES OF SCALE (2)	F-RATIO	SAMPLE SIZE
MIDDLE ATLANTIC	2.07	.47* (2.97)	.61* (5.32)	1.08 (1.18)	218.68	56.
NEW ENGLAND	3.91	.73* (8.91)	.34* (5.00)	1.07 (1.82)	422.69	65.
PACIFIC	.75	.05 (.26)	.91* (7.08)	.96 (-.31)	49.46	25.
SOUTHERN	.56	.06 (.61)	.89* (12.13)	.95 (-1.07)	286.13	109.
WESTERN	.65	.08 (.59)	.84* (8.79)	.92 (-1.35)	229.40	93.
THE UNITED STATES	1.28	.21* (4.02)	.76* (18.41)	.98 (-.78)	931.97	348.

FOOTNOTES --
(1) THE COEFFICIENT IS COMPARED TO A VALUE OF ZERO FOR TESTS OF SIGNIFICANCE
(2) THE COEFFICIENT IS COMPARED TO A VALUE OF ONE FOR TESTS OF SIGNIFICANCE
* COEFFICIENT SIGNIFICANTLY GREATER THAN ZERO (ONE) AT THE FIVE PERCENT LEVEL
** COEFFICIENT SIGNIFICANTLY LESS THAN ZERO (ONE) AT THE FIVE PERCENT LEVEL
REGIONS NOT APPEARING ABOVE MET ONE OF TWO CONDITIONS . . .
  (1) SAMPLE SIZE SMALLER THAN TWELVE, OR
  (2) NO SAMPLE FOR THE REGION (SEE TABLE 3.1)
REGIONS AS DESCRIBED IN THE TEXT

APPENDIX A.25

ORDINARY LEAST SQUARES ESTIMATES OF THE PRODUCTION FUNCTION FOR INDUSTRY SIC GROUP 20
CENSUS YEAR 1870
(T-RATIO)

REGION	INTERCEPT TERM	COEFFICIENT OF LABOR CAPITAL (1) (1)	ECONOMIES OF SCALE (2)	F-RATIO	SAMPLE SIZE
MIDDLE ATLANTIC	3.38	.69* .45* (6.57) (5.48)	1.13 (1.40)	71.31	73.
NEW ENGLAND	.78	.46* .73* (4.44) (8.19)	1.19* (2.63)	148.25	77.
PACIFIC	1.63	.29 .72* (1.69) (7.18)	1.01 (.08)	47.45	62.
SOUTHERN	.61	.50* .78* (6.95) (17.54)	1.28* (4.11)	274.62	482.
WESTERN	2.54	.75* .53* (4.50) (5.26)	1.27* (2.08)	60.24	87.
THE UNITED STATES	1.06	.49* .72* (10.26) (24.04)	1.21* (5.30)	691.47	781.

FOOTNOTES --
(1) THE COEFFICIENT IS COMPARED TO A VALUE OF ZERO FOR TESTS OF SIGNIFICANCE
(2) THE COEFFICIENT IS COMPARED TO A VALUE OF ONE FOR TESTS OF SIGNIFICANCE
* COEFFICIENT SIGNIFICANTLY GREATER THAN ZERO (ONE) AT THE FIVE PERCENT LEVEL
** COEFFICIENT SIGNIFICANTLY LESS THAN ZERO (ONE) AT THE FIVE PERCENT LEVEL
REGIONS NOT APPEARING ABOVE MET ONE OF TWO CONDITIONS . . .
  (1) SAMPLE SIZE SMALLER THAN TWELVE, OR
  (2) NO SAMPLE FOR THE REGION (SEE TABLE 3.1)
REGIONS AS DESCRIBED IN THE TEXT

APPENDIX A.26

ORDINARY LEAST SQUARES ESTIMATES OF THE PRODUCTION FUNCTION FOR INDUSTRY SIC GROUP 21
CENSUS YEAR 1870
(T-RATIO)

REGION	INTERCEPT TERM	COEFFICIENT OF LABOR (1)	COEFFICIENT OF CAPITAL (1)	ECONOMIES OF SCALE (2)	F-RATIO	SAMPLE SIZE
MIDDLE ATLANTIC	2.74	.35* (2.77)	.58* (5.91)	.93 (-.71)	54.19	28.
SOUTHERN	-1.02	-.34 (-1.38)	1.15* (5.57)	.81 (-1.40)	32.14	26.
WESTERN	2.91	.43* (4.03)	.53* (5.95)	.96 (-.71)	133.17	18.
THE UNITED STATES	1.42	.12 (1.31)	.77* (9.67)	.89 (-1.93)	136.21	83.

FOOTNOTES --
(1) THE COEFFICIENT IS COMPARED TO A VALUE OF ZERO FOR TESTS OF SIGNIFICANCE
(2) THE COEFFICIENT IS COMPARED TO A VALUE OF ONE FOR TESTS OF SIGNIFICANCE
* COEFFICIENT SIGNIFICANTLY GREATER THAN ZERO (ONE) AT THE FIVE PERCENT LEVEL
** COEFFICIENT SIGNIFICANTLY LESS THAN ZERO (ONE) AT THE FIVE PERCENT LEVEL
REGIONS NOT APPEARING ABOVE MET ONE OF TWO CONDITIONS . . .
  (1) SAMPLE SIZE SMALLER THAN TWELVE, OR
  (2) NO SAMPLE FOR THE REGION (SEE TABLE 3.1)
REGIONS AS DESCRIBED IN THE TEXT

APPENDIX A.27

ORDINARY LEAST SQUARES ESTIMATES OF THE PRODUCTION FUNCTION FOR INDUSTRY SIC GROUP 22
CENSUS YEAR 1870
(T-RATIO)

REGION	INTERCEPT TERM	COEFFICIENT OF LABOR CAPITAL (1)	ECONOMIES OF SCALE (2)	F-RATIO	SAMPLE SIZE
NEW ENGLAND	6.62	.96* .00 (4.92) (.01)	.96 (-.64)	111.93	31.
SOUTHERN	1.92	.52* .55* (2.35) (2.31)	1.07 (.57)	43.68	27.
THE UNITED STATES	2.41	.51* .52* (3.74) (4.24)	1.03 (.62)	241.53	72.

FOOTNOTES --
(1) THE COEFFICIENT IS COMPARED TO A VALUE OF ZERO FOR TESTS OF SIGNIFICANCE
(2) THE COEFFICIENT IS COMPARED TO A VALUE OF ONE FOR TESTS OF SIGNIFICANCE
 * COEFFICIENT SIGNIFICANTLY GREATER THAN ZERO (ONE) AT THE FIVE PERCENT LEVEL
 ** COEFFICIENT SIGNIFICANTLY LESS THAN ZERO (ONE) AT THE FIVE PERCENT LEVEL
REGIONS NOT APPEARING ABOVE MET ONE OF TWO CONDITIONS . . .
    (1) SAMPLE SIZE SMALLER THAN TWELVE, OR
    (2) NO SAMPLE FOR THE REGION (SEE TABLE 3.1)
REGIONS AS DESCRIBED IN THE TEXT

APPENDIX A.28

ORDINARY LEAST SQUARES ESTIMATES OF THE PRODUCTION FUNCTION FOR INDUSTRY SIC GROUP 23
CENSUS YEAR 1870
(T-RATIO)

REGION	INTERCEPT TERM	COEFFICIENT OF LABOR CAPITAL (1) (1)	ECONOMIES OF SCALE (2)	F-RATIO	SAMPLE SIZE
MIDDLE ATLANTIC	1.74	.32* .70* (2.47) (6.51)	1.03 (.35)	126.40	33.
NEW ENGLAND	1.66	.33* .68* (3.03) (7.22)	1.01 (.20)	178.16	56.
PACIFIC	1.85	.20 .76* (1.92) (6.82)	.96 (-.32)	37.81	26.
SOUTHERN	3.99	.46* .34* (3.01) (3.06)	.81 (-1.54)	22.51	59.
WESTERN	1.09	.16 .79* (1.23) (6.14)	.95 (-.82)	124.46	38.
THE UNITED STATES	2.28	.36* .61* (6.35) (11.99)	.98 (-.65)	392.92	212.

FOOTNOTES --
(1) THE COEFFICIENT IS COMPARED TO A VALUE OF ZERO FOR TESTS OF SIGNIFICANCE
(2) THE COEFFICIENT IS COMPARED TO A VALUE OF ONE FOR TESTS OF SIGNIFICANCE
* COEFFICIENT SIGNIFICANTLY GREATER THAN ZERO (ONE) AT THE FIVE PERCENT LEVEL
** COEFFICIENT SIGNIFICANTLY LESS THAN ZERO (ONE) AT THE FIVE PERCENT LEVEL
REGIONS NOT APPEARING ABOVE MET ONE OF TWO CONDITIONS . . .
  (1) SAMPLE SIZE SMALLER THAN TWELVE, OR
  (2) NO SAMPLE FOR THE REGION (SEE TABLE 3.1)
REGIONS AS DESCRIBED IN THE TEXT

APPENDIX A.29

ORDINARY LEAST SQUARES ESTIMATES OF THE PRODUCTION FUNCTION FOR INDUSTRY SIC GROUP 24
CENSUS YEAR 1870
(T-RATIO)

REGION	INTERCEPT TERM	COEFFICIENT OF LABOR CAPITAL (1)		ECONOMIES OF SCALE (2)	F-RATIO	SAMPLE SIZE
MIDDLE ATLANTIC	.04	.31* (2.26)	.86* (7.12)	1.17 (1.37)	53.15	52.
NEW ENGLAND	1.00	.36* (5.13)	.71* (12.07)	1.08* (2.19)	573.50	185.
PACIFIC	1.97	.44* (3.55)	.64* (6.19)	1.08 (1.20)	166.82	70.
SOUTHERN	1.20	.50* (6.94)	.70* (12.13)	1.20* (4.02)	338.05	312.
WESTERN	1.40	.22* (2.03)	.72* (8.50)	.94 (-1.02)	201.01	122.
THE UNITED STATES	1.34	.40* (10.21)	.69* (21.68)	1.10* (3.84)	1157.53	741.

FOOTNOTES --
(1) THE COEFFICIENT IS COMPARED TO A VALUE OF ZERO FOR TESTS OF SIGNIFICANCE
(2) THE COEFFICIENT IS COMPARED TO A VALUE OF ONE FOR TESTS OF SIGNIFICANCE
* COEFFICIENT SIGNIFICANTLY GREATER THAN ZERO (ONE) AT THE FIVE PERCENT LEVEL
** COEFFICIENT SIGNIFICANTLY LESS THAN ZERO (ONE) AT THE FIVE PERCENT LEVEL
REGIONS NOT APPEARING ABOVE MET ONE OF TWO CONDITIONS . . .
(1) SAMPLE SIZE SMALLER THAN TWELVE, OR
(2) NO SAMPLE FOR THE REGION (SEE TABLE 3.1)
REGIONS AS DESCRIBED IN THE TEXT

APPENDIX A.30

ORDINARY LEAST SQUARES ESTIMATES OF THE PRODUCTION FUNCTION FOR INDUSTRY SIC GROUP 25
CENSUS YEAR 1870
(T-RATIO)

REGION	INTERCEPT TERM	COEFFICIENT OF LABOR CAPITAL (1) (1)	ECONOMIES OF SCALE (2)	F-RATIO	SAMPLE SIZE
MIDDLE ATLANTIC	-.24	-.12 1.01* (-.27) (2.56)	.89 (-.62)	17.50	19.
NEW ENGLAND	2.51	.26 .61* (1.32) (2.87)	.87 (-1.20)	33.03	17.
SOUTHERN	3.35	.48* .50* (2.28) (3.15)	.98 (-.24)	97.17	31.
WESTERN	.42	.03 .90* (.12) (4.74)	.93 (-.71)	50.02	24.
THE UNITED STATES	2.30	.24* .65* (2.29) (7.06)	.90** (-2.11)	195.97	98.

FOOTNOTES --
(1) THE COEFFICIENT IS COMPARED TO A VALUE OF ZERO FOR TESTS OF SIGNIFICANCE
(2) THE COEFFICIENT IS COMPARED TO A VALUE OF ONE FOR TESTS OF SIGNIFICANCE
* COEFFICIENT SIGNIFICANTLY GREATER THAN ZERO (ONE) AT THE FIVE PERCENT LEVEL
** COEFFICIENT SIGNIFICANTLY LESS THAN ZERO (ONE) AT THE FIVE PERCENT LEVEL
REGIONS NOT APPEARING ABOVE MET ONE OF TWO CONDITIONS . . .
 (1) SAMPLE SIZE SMALLER THAN TWELVE, OR
 (2) NO SAMPLE FOR THE REGION (SEE TABLE 3.1)
REGIONS AS DESCRIBED IN THE TEXT

APPENDIX A.31

ORDINARY LEAST SQUARES ESTIMATES OF THE PRODUCTION FUNCTION FOR INDUSTRY SIC GROUP 28
CENSUS YEAR 1870
(T-RATIO)

REGION	INTERCEPT TERM	COEFFICIENT OF LABOR CAPITAL (1) (1)	ECONOMIES OF SCALE (2)	F-RATIO	SAMPLE SIZE
SOUTHERN	3.94	.39 .33 (.89) (1.28)	.72 (-1.16)	11.88	18.
THE UNITED STATES	3.19	.38 .47* (1.44) (3.11)	.85 (-1.03)	41.94	36.

FOOTNOTES --
(1) THE COEFFICIENT IS COMPARED TO A VALUE OF ZERO FOR TESTS OF SIGNIFICANCE
(2) THE COEFFICIENT IS COMPARED TO A VALUE OF ONE FOR TESTS OF SIGNIFICANCE
* COEFFICIENT SIGNIFICANTLY GREATER THAN ZERO (ONE) AT THE FIVE PERCENT LEVEL
** COEFFICIENT SIGNIFICANTLY LESS THAN ZERO (ONE) AT THE FIVE PERCENT LEVEL
REGIONS NOT APPEARING ABOVE MET ONE OF TWO CONDITIONS . . .
  (1) SAMPLE SIZE SMALLER THAN TWELVE, OR
  (2) NO SAMPLE FOR THE REGION (SEE TABLE 3.1)
REGIONS AS DESCRIBED IN THE TEXT

APPENDIX A.32

ORDINARY LEAST SQUARES ESTIMATES OF THE PRODUCTION FUNCTION FOR INDUSTRY SIC GROUP 31
CENSUS YEAR 1870
(T-RATIO)

REGION	INTERCEPT TERM	COEFFICIENT OF LABOR (1)	COEFFICIENT OF CAPITAL (1)	ECONOMIES OF SCALE (2)	F-RATIO	SAMPLE SIZE
MIDDLE ATLANTIC	3.67	.46* (4.90)	.47* (8.05)	.94 (-1.12)	257.77	92.
NEW ENGLAND	2.50	.35* (3.98)	.60* (8.37)	.95 (-1.20)	311.34	120.
PACIFIC	3.29	.47* (3.27)	.52* (5.04)	.99 (-.09)	44.72	44.
SOUTHERN	3.35	.50* (4.17)	.46* (6.69)	.96 (-.52)	105.65	217.
WESTERN	2.75	.34* (2.57)	.56* (6.45)	.90 (-1.21)	89.82	111.
THE UNITED STATES	3.03	.42* (8.22)	.53* (15.28)	.94 (-1.85)	742.89	584.

FOOTNOTES --
(1) THE COEFFICIENT IS COMPARED TO A VALUE OF ZERO FOR TESTS OF SIGNIFICANCE
(2) THE COEFFICIENT IS COMPARED TO A VALUE OF ONE FOR TESTS OF SIGNIFICANCE
* COEFFICIENT SIGNIFICANTLY GREATER THAN ZERO (ONE) AT THE FIVE PERCENT LEVEL
** COEFFICIENT SIGNIFICANTLY LESS THAN ZERO (ONE) AT THE FIVE PERCENT LEVEL
REGIONS NOT APPEARING ABOVE MET ONE OF TWO CONDITIONS . . .
  (1) SAMPLE SIZE SMALLER THAN TWELVE, OR
  (2) NO SAMPLE FOR THE REGION (SEE TABLE 3.1)
REGIONS AS DESCRIBED IN THE TEXT

APPENDIX A.33

ORDINARY LEAST SQUARES ESTIMATES OF THE PRODUCTION FUNCTION FOR INDUSTRY SIC GROUP 33
CENSUS YEAR 1870
(T-RATIO)

REGION	INTERCEPT TERM	COEFFICIENT OF LABOR CAPITAL (1)	ECONOMIES OF SCALE (2)	F-RATIO	SAMPLE SIZE
MIDDLE ATLANTIC	3.33	.56* .46* (2.39) (2.75)	1.02 (.17)	53.37	16.
NEW ENGLAND	1.77	.24 .70* (1.41) (5.41)	.93 (-.91)	146.17	23.
SOUTHERN	-.45	-.22 .98* (-.73) (4.50)	.76 (-1.78)	44.15	20.
THE UNITED STATES	1.56	.22 .70* (1.70) (7.26)	.92 (-1.24)	196.11	71.

FOOTNOTES --
(1) THE COEFFICIENT IS COMPARED TO A VALUE OF ZERO FOR TESTS OF SIGNIFICANCE
(2) THE COEFFICIENT IS COMPARED TO A VALUE OF ONE FOR TESTS OF SIGNIFICANCE
* COEFFICIENT SIGNIFICANTLY GREATER THAN ZERO (ONE) AT THE FIVE PERCENT LEVEL
** COEFFICIENT SIGNIFICANTLY LESS THAN ZERO (ONE) AT THE FIVE PERCENT LEVEL
REGIONS NOT APPEARING ABOVE MET ONE OF TWO CONDITIONS . . .
  (1) SAMPLE SIZE SMALLER THAN TWELVE, OR
  (2) NO SAMPLE FOR THE REGION (SEE TABLE 3.1)
REGIONS AS DESCRIBED IN THE TEXT

APPENDIX A.34

ORDINARY LEAST SQUARES ESTIMATES OF THE PRODUCTION FUNCTION FOR INDUSTRY SIC GROUP 34
CENSUS YEAR 1870
(T-RATIO)

REGION	INTERCEPT TERM	COEFFICIENT OF LABOR (1)	CAPITAL (1)	ECONOMIES OF SCALE (2)	F-RATIO	SAMPLE SIZE
MIDDLE ATLANTIC	1.76	.35 (1.49)	.71* (3.66)	1.07 (.69)	87.21	22.
NEW ENGLAND	3.42	.53* (4.33)	.46* (4.42)	.98 (-.35)	290.19	50.
SOUTHERN	3.18	.46* (2.16)	.49* (3.37)	.96 (-.28)	28.73	40.
WESTERN	2.82	.43 (1.49)	.53* (2.67)	.96 (-.33)	55.81	30.
THE UNITED STATES	2.83	.43* (4.63)	.55* (7.56)	.97 (-.65)	380.98	150.

FOOTNOTES --
(1) THE COEFFICIENT IS COMPARED TO A VALUE OF ZERO FOR TESTS OF SIGNIFICANCE
(2) THE COEFFICIENT IS COMPARED TO A VALUE OF ONE FOR TESTS OF SIGNIFICANCE
* COEFFICIENT SIGNIFICANTLY GREATER THAN ZERO (ONE) AT THE FIVE PERCENT LEVEL
** COEFFICIENT SIGNIFICANTLY LESS THAN ZERO (ONE) AT THE FIVE PERCENT LEVEL
REGIONS NOT APPEARING ABOVE MET ONE OF TWO CONDITIONS . . .
(1) SAMPLE SIZE SMALLER THAN TWELVE, OR
(2) NO SAMPLE FOR THE REGION (SEE TABLE 3.1)
REGIONS AS DESCRIBED IN THE TEXT

APPENDIX A.35

ORDINARY LEAST SQUARES ESTIMATES OF THE PRODUCTION FUNCTION FOR INDUSTRY SIC GROUP 35
CENSUS YEAR 1870
(T-RATIO)

REGION	INTERCEPT TERM	COEFFICIENT OF LABOR CAPITAL (1)	ECONOMIES OF SCALE (2)	F-RATIO	SAMPLE SIZE
NEW ENGLAND	3.58	.74* .38 (2.40) (1.29)	1.12 (1.06)	48.53	20.
THE UNITED STATES	2.09	.38* .64* (2.90) (5.89)	1.02 (.25)	162.78	51.

FOOTNOTES --
(1) THE COEFFICIENT IS COMPARED TO A VALUE OF ZERO FOR TESTS OF SIGNIFICANCE
(2) THE COEFFICIENT IS COMPARED TO A VALUE OF ONE FOR TESTS OF SIGNIFICANCE
* COEFFICIENT SIGNIFICANTLY GREATER THAN ZERO (ONE) AT THE FIVE PERCENT LEVEL
** COEFFICIENT SIGNIFICANTLY LESS THAN ZERO (ONE) AT THE FIVE PERCENT LEVEL
REGIONS NOT APPEARING ABOVE MET ONE OF TWO CONDITIONS . . .
    (1) SAMPLE SIZE SMALLER THAN TWELVE, OR
    (2) NO SAMPLE FOR THE REGION (SEE TABLE 3.1)
REGIONS AS DESCRIBED IN THE TEXT

APPENDIX A.36

ORDINARY LEAST SQUARES ESTIMATES OF THE PRODUCTION FUNCTION FOR INDUSTRY SIC GROUP 37
CENSUS YEAR 1870
(T-RATIO)

REGION	INTERCEPT TERM	COEFFICIENT OF LABOR CAPITAL (1) (1)	ECONOMIES OF SCALE (2)	F-RATIO	SAMPLE SIZE
MIDDLE ATLANTIC	4.14	.63* .34 (2.53) (1.53)	.97 (-.47)	206.06	23.
NEW ENGLAND	1.83	.32* .69* (2.82) (7.25)	1.01 (.13)	207.00	57.
PACIFIC	1.06	.15 .79* (.79) (4.59)	.95 (-.55)	58.45	32.
SOUTHERN	1.63	.06 .74* (1.17) (14.51)	.80** (-4.73)	213.53	96.
WESTERN	-.31	-.02 .97* (-1.04) (24.76)	.94 (-1.55)	343.24	40.
THE UNITED STATES	.92	.04 .83* (1.50) (29.58)	.87** (-5.49)	822.14	248.

FOOTNOTES --
(1) THE COEFFICIENT IS COMPARED TO A VALUE OF ZERO FOR TESTS OF SIGNIFICANCE
(2) THE COEFFICIENT IS COMPARED TO A VALUE OF ONE FOR TESTS OF SIGNIFICANCE
* COEFFICIENT SIGNIFICANTLY GREATER THAN ZERO (ONE) AT THE FIVE PERCENT LEVEL
** COEFFICIENT SIGNIFICANTLY LESS THAN ZERO (ONE) AT THE FIVE PERCENT LEVEL
REGIONS NOT APPEARING ABOVE MET ONE OF TWO CONDITIONS . . . .
   (1) SAMPLE SIZE SMALLER THAN TWELVE, OR
   (2) NO SAMPLE FOR THE REGION (SEE TABLE 3.1)
REGIONS AS DESCRIBED IN THE TEXT